"Sometimes a book is so impo̶̶̶̶̶̶̶̶̶̶̶̶̶̶̶̶̶̶̶̶̶ ave read it is to embarrass oneself ̶̶̶̶̶̶̶̶ message is so crucial and so clear that all Americans are obligated to read it and have a national conversation on its themes. No cultural commentator or politician who has not read this book should ever be taken seriously again. Let this book be the new litmus test. If you are serious about America, be familiar with its themes and expect to discuss them and to be tested on them. Rest assured that you will be, because America is now herself being tested on them. Alas, we will not be graded on a curve. This book's clarion call is both piercing and full of hope. May God help us to hear it and to take action."

ERIC METAXAS, *New York Times* best-selling author of *Bonhoeffer: Pastor, Martyr, Prophet, Spy* and *Amazing Grace: William Wilberforce and the Heroic Campaign to End Slavery*

"Os Guinness enlightens, cheers, chastises and informs with this latest contribution to our civic discourse. Guinness here solidifies his reputation as one of the most nimble voices from the Christian community as he surveys our history and our present with appreciation as well as deep concern. Highly recommended for all interested citizens, whatever their political or faith commitments."

JEAN BETHKE ELSHTAIN, Laura Spelman Rockefeller Professor of Social and Political Ethics at the University of Chicago, author of *Sovereignty: God, State and Self*

"With passion and urgency Os Guinness gives a sweeping historical account of America's past and her prospects for the future. He urges us to pay serious attention to a deeper understanding of freedom and makes a compelling case for why freedom requires virtue. Weaving together a wide-ranging knowledge of classical, constitutional and contemporary history, Guinness warns of America's decline but charts a course for America's renewal. It is a straight-shooting and sober volume, yet in the end it is a hopeful book."

MICHAEL CROMARTIE, vice president, Ethics and Public Policy Center, Washington, D.C.

"In a passionate work that blends historical-cultural analysis with moral exhortation, Os Guinness finds at the heart of America's culture wars something different than what many observers have seen there. He identifies a 'freedom war,' a struggle over the very concept of freedom itself, in which a new and open-ended sense of the term threatens to engulf all older meanings. As the Founders well understood, it is not enough for Americans to invoke endlessly the name of 'freedom' when they no longer agree as to what it means, and particularly when they have lost an understanding of the preconditions of freedom, as well as the ends freedom is meant to serve. Guinness warns that freedom cannot long endure unless it is consecrated to purposes beyond itself. It is a warning worth heeding."

WILFRED M. MCCLAY, SunTrust Chair of Excellence in Humanities, University of Tennessee at Chattanooga, and author of *The Masterless: Self and Society in Modern America*

"*A Free People's Suicide* is an inside view from the outside. Os Guinness has a clear eye, a quick mind, a profound grasp of political philosophy and an eloquent pen. His analysis of American freedom, what it has been, now is and is likely to become, is a clarion call for renewal of the Founders' vision for a free people."

JAMES W. SIRE, author of *The Universe Next Door* and *Václav Havel: The Intellectual Conscience of International Politics*

A FREE
PEOPLE'S
SUICIDE

Sustainable Freedom
and the
American Future

OS GUINNESS

IVP Books

An imprint of InterVarsity Press
Downers Grove, Illinois

InterVarsity Press
P.O. Box 1400, Downers Grove, IL 60515-1426
World Wide Web: www.ivpress.com
E-mail: email@ivpress.com

InterVarsity Press® is the book-publishing division of InterVarsity Christian Fellowship/USA®, a
movement of students and faculty active on campus at hundreds of universities, colleges and schools
of nursing in the United States of America, and a member movement of the International Fellowship
of Evangelical Students. For information about local and regional activities, write Public Relations
Dept., InterVarsity Christian Fellowship/USA, 6400 Schroeder Rd., P.O. Box 7895, Madison, WI
53707-7895, or visit the IVCF website at <www.intervarsity.org>.

All Scripture quotations, unless otherwise indicated, are taken from the Holy Bible, New
International Version®. NIV®. Copyright ©1973, 1978, 1984 by International Bible Society. Used by
permission of Zondervan Publishing House. All rights reserved.

Every effort has been made to credit all material quoted in this book. Any errors or omissions brought
to the publisher's attention will be corrected in future editions.

Published in association with the literary agency of Wolgemuth & Associates.

Cover design: Cindy Kiple
Images: Stained American flag: © Hande Guleryuz Yuce/iStockphoto
        Declaration of Independence signatures: © Duncan Walker/iStockphoto
        eagle: © Alisher Burhonov/iStockphoto

ISBN 978-0-8308-3465-5

Printed in the United States of America ∞

Library of Congress Cataloging-in-Publication Data

Guinness, Os.
  A free people's suicide: sustainable freedom and the American
future / Os Guinness.
      p. cm.
  Includes bibliographical references (p.   ).
  ISBN 978-8308-3465-5 (pbk.: alk. paper)
  1. Liberty—Religious aspects—Christianity. 2.
  Christianity—United States—21st century. 3. United States—Politics
  and government—21st century. 4. United States—Forecasting. I.
  Title
  BR517.G85 2012
  261.70973—dc23

                                                              2012015955

P   18   17   16   15   14   13   12   11   10   9   8   7   6   5   4   3   2

Y   27   26   25   24   23   22   21   20   19   18   17   16   15   14   13   12

To Bud and Jane Smith,

dear friends and great American patriots

MARCUS TULLIUS CICERO

The preservation of the republic no less than governing it—What a thankless task it is!

—Speech, November 6, 63 B.C.

But our age, having received the commonwealth as a finished picture of another century, but already beginning to fade through the lapse of years, has not only neglected to renew the colors of the original painting, but has not even cared to preserve its original form and prominent lineaments.

For what now remains of those antique manners, of which the poet said that our commonwealth consisted? They have now become obsolete and forgotten, that they are not only cultivated, but they are not even known. . . . For it is owing to our vices, rather than to any accident, that we have retained the name of republic when we have long since lost the reality.

—On the Republic

AUGUSTINE OF HIPPO

Suppose we were to define what it means to be a people not in the usual way, but in a different fashion such as the following: a people is a multitudinous assemblage of rational beings united by concord regarding loved things held in common. Then, if we wished to discern the character of any given people, we would have to investigate what it loves. . . . Surely it is a better or worse people as it is united in loving things that are better or worse.

—City of God

CHARLES LOUIS DE SECONDAT, BARON DE MONTESQUIEU

Just as all human things come to an end, the state of which we speak will lose its liberty; it will perish. Rome, Lacedaemon & Carthage have in fact perished. This state will perish when the legislative will be more corrupt than the executive power.

—Spirit of Laws

BENJAMIN FRANKLIN

Nothing brings more pain than too much pleasure; nothing more bondage than too much liberty.

—Poor Richard's Almanac

JOHN ADAMS

A memorable epoch in the annals of the human race destined in history to form the brightest or the blackest page, according to the use or abuse of those political institutions by which they shall in time come to be shaped by the human mind.

—Letter in 1826 on the outcome of 1776

GEORGE WASHINGTON

It is yet to be decided whether the Revolution must ultimately be considered a blessing or a curse: a blessing or a curse, not to the present age alone, for with our fate will the destiny of unborn Millions be involved. . . . At this auspicious period, the United States came into existence as a Nation, and if their Citizens should not be completely free and happy, the fault will be entirely their own.

—"Circular to the States," Newburgh, New York, 1783

JAMES MADISON

Liberty may be endangered by the abuses of liberty as well as the abuses of power.

—The Federalist

ALEXIS DE TOCQUEVILLE

[We should not comfort ourselves] on the supposition that the barbarians are still far from us, for there are people who allow the light to be snatched from their hands, and there are other peoples who stifle it under their own feet.

—Democracy in America

ABRAHAM LINCOLN

At what point then is the approach of danger to be expected? I answer, if it ever reach us, it must spring up among us. It cannot come from abroad. If destruction be our lot, we must ourselves be its author and finisher. As a nation of freemen, we must live through all time, or die by suicide.

—"Address Before the Young Men's Lyceum," Springfield, Illinois, 1838

LORD MOULTON

The greatness of a nation, its true civilization, is measured by the extent of its obedience to the unenforceable.

—The Atlantic

THEODORE ROOSEVELT

We must keep steadily in mind that no people were ever yet benefited by riches if their prosperity corrupted their virtue.

—Speech, July 4, 1886, North Dakota

ALBERT CAMUS

Freedom is not a reward or a decoration that is celebrated with champagne. Nor yet a gift, a box of dainties designed to make you lick your chops. Oh no, it's a chore . . . and a long distance race, quite solitary and very exhausting.

—The Fall

DWIGHT D. EISENHOWER

How far can you go without destroying from within what you are trying to defend from without?

JOHN W. GARDNER

It is by means of the free society that we keep ourselves free. If we wish to remain free, we had better look to the health, the vigor, the viability of our free society—and to its capacity for renewal.

—Self-Renewal

JOSEPH BRODSKY

A free man, when he fails, blames nobody.

—"The Condition We Call Exile"

Contents

1

What Kind of People Do You Think You Are?

There is always a moment in the story of great powers when their own citizens become their own worst enemies—not so much in the form of homegrown terrorism as in the form of the citizenry thinking and living at odds with what it takes for the nation to thrive. What follows is a visitor's perspective on how America is reaching that point today and on what can be done to restore the American republic to its vitality before it's too late.

THE SIFTING OF HISTORY

The day after Christmas would normally have been a quiet day in Washington, D.C., above all on Capitol Hill. But December 26, 1941, was different. It was only nineteen days after the Japanese attack on Pearl Harbor, and both the Senate chamber and the overflow gallery were packed to hear British Prime Minister Winston Churchill address a joint session of the United States Congress.

With the Capitol ringed by police and soldiers, the lectern bristling with microphones, and the glare of unusually bright lights in the chamber for the film cameras, Churchill started his thirty-minute address with a light touch. "If my father had been an American," he said, "and my mother British, instead of the other way around, I might have gotten here on my own. In that case this would not have been the first time you would have heard my voice." Churchill then rose to his central theme. Britain was standing alone, but reeling. Most of Europe lay prostrate under the Nazi heel. Hitler was well on his way to Moscow. Half of the American Navy was at the bottom of the Hawaiian harbor, and there was little or no air force to rise to the nation's defense. He therefore delivered a stern denunciation of the Japanese and the German menace, and warned about "the many disappointments and unpleasant surprises that await us" in countering them.

At the heart of the prime minister's address was a famous question to his listeners in light of the Japanese aggression: "What kind of a people do they think we are? Is it possible that they do not realize that we shall never cease to persevere against them until they have been taught a lesson which they and the world will never forget?"[1]

All crises are judgments of history that call into question an existing state of affairs. They sift and sort the character and condition of a nation and its capacity to respond. The deeper the crisis, the more serious the sifting and the deeper the questions it raises. At the very least, a crisis raises the question "What should we do?" Without that, it would not amount to a crisis.

Deeper crises raise the deeper question "Where are we, and how did we get here?" Still deeper crises raise the question Churchill raised, "Who do *other people* think we are?"—though clearly Churchill saw the ignorance in the Japanese mind, rather than in his or his hearers'. But the deepest crises of all are those that raise the question "Who do *we* think we are?" when doubt and uncertainty have entered our own thinking.

This last question poses a challenge and requires a courage that goes to the very heart of the identity and character of those in crisis, whether individuals or a nation. Only in a response that clearly says and shows who they are can they demonstrate an answer that resolves the crisis constructively and answers history's judgment by turning potential danger into an opportunity for growth and advance. History is asking that last question of America now: *What kind of a people do you Americans think you are?* We are now nearly eight decades after the Great Depression, seven decades after Pearl Harbor and World War II, four decades after the tumultuous and influential sixties, two decades after the collapse of the Soviet Union and the bipolar world, one decade after September 11 and in the midst of two of the most revealing and fateful presidencies in American history. The sifting of America has come to a head, and the question "Who are you?" or "What kind of a people do *you* think you are?" or "What kind of society do you want America to be" is now the central question Americans must answer.

Another time of testing has come. Another day of reckoning is here. This is a testing and a reckoning—let me say it carefully— that could prove even more decisive than earlier trials such as the Civil War, the Depression and the cultural cataclysm that was the 1960s. As citizens of the world's lead society and leaders of Western civilization, you Americans owe yourselves and the world a clear answer at this momentous juncture of your history and international leadership—a moment at which an unclear answer or no answer at all are both a clear answer and a telling symptom of the judgment of history.

There are many reasons Americans must answer the question "Who do you think you are?" The widely watched drama of the recent political crisis over the debt ceiling and the deeply felt consequences of the economic crisis, the continuing unemployment and the mounting social inequities have made them the most discussed issues at the moment—with concerns trumpeted by the Tea Party movement on one side and the Occupy Wall Street protest on the other.

These issues pale, however, when compared with the challenge facing America at the prospect of the ending of the five-hundred-year dominance of the West and the emergence of an Asia-led world. And all these issues together are just the beginning of a mounting sea of problems engulfing America from many sides. But this book addresses a neglected issue that may prove the deepest and most urgent of all, if only because it is intertwined with so many of the others: the gathering crisis of *sustainable freedom in America.*

At his inauguration President Obama faced a scale and range of problems that were unprecedented in recent memory. What was less noted and more important was that most of these problems raised questions that go to the heart of the American republic, and foreign admirers of America are disappointed to see America failing to live up to its past and its potential in these problem areas. In short, the state of the Union is at stake.

Let me introduce the claim that America's deepest crisis is the crisis of sustainable freedom by setting out a number of simple points that have converged to make it urgent.

AMERICA'S GLORY AND
SUPREME LOVE

First, sustainable freedom is urgent for America because freedom is, and will always be, the issue of all issues for America. In today's world, it is customary to assess nations in terms of the size of their population, the strength of their economy, the power and reach of their armed forces, the state of their information technology, the prestige of their research universities and so on. But there is a deeper classical way to see things: it was once understood that every nation has its own special character, its own animating principle, and can be understood and assessed only in that light.

Augustine of Hippo argued that the best way to define a people is by their "loved thing held in common," or what it is they love supremely. A people can be judged as better or worse according to what they love, and their nation can be assessed as healthy or unhealthy according to the condition of what they love. Freedom is unquestionably what Americans love supremely, and love of freedom is what makes Americans the people they are. Thus the present crisis of sustainable freedom raises questions about the health of the American republic that must be taken seriously.[2]

Freedom is so central and precious to Americans that it might seem odd, and even outrageous, for an outsider to challenge Americans over their freedom. But this book is not a sour foreign attack on American freedom. I am a long-time admirer of the American experiment and of the place of freedom in America. Unquestionably freedom is, and will always be, America's animating principle and chief glory, her most important idea and her greatest strength.

But unless sustained, freedom could also prove to be America's idol—something trusted ultimately that cannot bear ultimate weight. Assessing the condition of freedom is therefore central to the promise and peril of America in the advanced modern world, just as it was to the success of the American Revolution.

For one thing, freedom is the special glory of America, the chief boast of Americans and the central reason for the importance of America for the democratic project, for the modern world and for humanity. From its very beginning, the United States was blessed with a sturdy birthright of freedom. It was born in freedom, it has expanded in freedom, it has resolved its great conflicts in a "new birth of freedom," it has won its spurs as a world power in defending freedom, and it now stands as the global colossus of freedom offering its gift to the world and announcing that, as freedom spreads, it will herald an era of peace between freedom-loving nations on earth.

Due largely to America, freedom is at the very heart and soul of the modern world, especially in its Western forms. In all the world's free-thought, free-speech, free-choice, free-vote, free-market societies, freedom is today's highest virtue, its grandest possibility, its last absolute, its most potent myth and—with the power of love

limited to the private world—its only self-evident public truth. How
else are modern people to be themselves other than to be free?

Freedom as the dream of ever-expanding emancipation, ever-
multiplying liberation movements and ever-deepening fulfillment is
being pushed from behind by the memory of a thousand oppressions
and pulled from ahead by the promise of unrestrained choice and
unhindered creativity leading to unlimited possibilities ("infinite in
all directions," as the futurist cheerleaders say). Unfettered freedom
could prove to be the Achilles' heel of the modern world, dissipating
into license, triviality, corruption and a grand undermining of all
authority, but for the moment the world is still both thrilled and en-
thralled by the great Age of Freedom. It is the Western world's most
stunning success, and the United States is its proudest exemplar.

No self-respecting American will ever be opposed to freedom any
more than to love. And it is incontestable that, in American history,
whoever represents "the party of freedom"—sometimes the Democrats, as under Franklin Roosevelt, and sometimes the Republicans,
as under Ronald Reagan—has always prevailed over any who appear
to be standing in its way.

THE GRAND PARADOX OF FREEDOM

Second, sustainable freedom is urgent for America because freedom
is far more difficult to sustain than most Americans realize. We live
at a time when words such as *freedom*, *progress* and *values* are
bandied around endlessly, yet few people stop to ask what they
mean, now that the last generation has seen them emptied of almost
all content.

Needless to say, America's espousal of freedom has never been
pure and undiluted. Jefferson hailed the United States as the "empire
of liberty" or an "empire for liberty such as she has never surveyed
since the creation."[3] Yet from the start, the empire of liberty was built
at the expense of African slaves, American Indians and American

women. But the perennial challenges to sustainable freedom go well beyond these long-standing contradictions so amply explored by historians since the 1960s.

The glory of freedom should never blind anyone to its immoderate nature and therefore to the stern requirements that surround it. For at the heart of freedom lies a grand paradox: *the greatest enemy of freedom is freedom.* Throughout the course of history, freedom presents an inescapable and tightly coiled conundrum that sums up the challenge of why it is so difficult to sustain. Stripped to its core dimensions, the conundrum may be stated as follows:

For a start, freedom always faces a fundamental historical challenge. Although glorious, free societies are few, far between and fleeting. In the past, the high view of human dignity and independence that free societies require was attained by only two societies with world influence: the Greeks with their view of the *logos*, or reason within each person, and the Jews with their notion of the call of God to each person. The Roman ways owed much to the Greeks, of course, just as contemporary humanists owe everything to the Jewish, Greek and Christian ideas from which they come and on which they depend.

Today's worldwide explosion of freedom is therefore rare and cannot be taken for granted. If the hundred-centuries clock of civilization is compressed to a single hour, today's interest in freedom and democracy appears only in the last minute or so before midnight, so to take it as the norm is folly.

Further, freedom faces a fundamental political challenge. Free societies must always maintain their freedom on two levels at once: at the level of their nation's constitution and at the level of their citizens' convictions. The formal structures of liberty and the informal spirit of liberty—or the fundamental laws and the fundamental "habits of the heart"—are both essential to freedom, though in different ways. If the structures of liberty are well built, they last as long as they are properly maintained, whereas the spirit of liberty and the habits of the heart must be reinvigorated from generation to generation. Conversely, whatever the strength of the structures of liberty, they may always be overrun in the end by the will of the people. Put differently, a nation's constitution is like a covenant, and there are always at least two parties to a covenant. A nation's constitution may therefore remain strong and clear, yet still be nullified by the citizenry failing to uphold its side of the covenant.

This distinction between the structures of liberty and the spirit of liberty—or between the laws and the habits of the heart—was less important to the Greeks because, as James Madison observed, theirs was a "pure democracy." There was no clear-cut difference between society and state, and their democracy consisted of "a small number of citizens who assemble and administer the government *in person*."[4] There was no Athens, only "the Athenians"—the entire citizenry in assembly, at war or in the creation of their immortal works of art such as the Acropolis and the tragedies of Aeschylus, Euripides and Sophocles.

But as the greatest European commentators have underscored, all societies in the modern world have a significant gap between society and state, so it is possible to be free at the constitutional level in terms of the structures of liberty but to lose freedom and become servile or anarchic at the citizens' level in terms of the spirit of liberty. Conversely, though less common, it is possible to exercise the spirit of liberty at the level of citizens without enjoying liberty at the level of the constitution. In Montesquieu's words, "It can happen that the constitution will be free & the citizen not" or that "the citizen will be free & the constitution not."[5]

Finally, freedom always faces a fundamental moral challenge. Freedom requires order and therefore restraint, yet the only restraint that does not contradict freedom is self-restraint, which is the very thing that freedom undermines when it flourishes. Thus the heart of the problem of freedom is the problem of the heart, because free societies are characterized by restlessness at their core.

Such a claim sounds pious, but it was argued by thinkers who were far from pious. Machiavelli, for example, rooted political restlessness in the fact that human appetites are by nature "insatiable" because human beings are "able to desire everything" but unable "to secure everything." As a result, "their desire is always greater than the power of acquisition."[6] Similarly, Montesquieu, who followed John Locke, who in turn followed Blaise Pascal, Pierre Nicole and Augustine (though with no interest in the theological concerns of the last three), described political restlessness as a chronic uneasiness that gives freedom-loving people an "uneasy spirit" and leaves them "always inflamed."[7] And all this in a day long before modern consumerism stoked the restlessness even further.

Put differently, the shining principle of the consent of the governed is at the heart of democracy and is crucial to both freedom and its legitimacy. But it is also beguiling because it masks a challenge. In a democratic republic, the rulers and the subjects are one and the same, so freedom depends constantly not only on the character of the nation's leaders but also on the character of its citizens.

Yet such are human passions and the political restlessness they create that the self-renunciation essential to the self-restraint needed for sustaining freedom is quite unnatural. It goes against the grain of humanness—especially in peaceful and prosperous periods, when there is no requirement to rise above private interests and remember the public good, and very especially in bitterly anxious times such as the present, when so many citizens contradict rather than consent to the government-that-is-them. We have now reached the point where no sooner do Americans send their representatives to Washington than they turn on the Washington that they claim no longer represents them.

The core problem can be expressed like this: Such is our human propensity for self-love—or thinking and acting with the self as center—that the virtue it takes for citizens to remain free is quite unnatural. America today is a republic in which the private trumps the public, consumerism tells Americans, "It's all about me," and citizens constantly tell the government to "get off our backs" when the government is their own justly chosen representative and it supposedly governs only with their free consent. In such a world, self-love will always love itself supremely, love itself at the expense of others and love itself without limits.

Thus, in Montesquieu's words, the self-renunciation needed for freedom is "always a very painful thing."[8] The natural bent of self-love is toward domination, not self-restraint, so the will to power at its heart will relentlessly seek to expand unless it meets resistance. Freedom therefore thrives on freedom and, mistaking power for freedom, expands naturally to produce the abuse of power that throttles freedom—that is, unless freedom is checked and balanced strongly, wisely and constantly.

If freedom is not checked in this way, and worse still, if it is defined only negatively (as freedom *from constraint*, as it is in much of America today), then assertive freedom will refuse to be checked by anyone and anything outside itself. It will then press instinctively for freedom from *all* outside constraints, whether from social conventions, long-standing traditions, rational criteria, moral standards or divine commandments, for they are all external constraints that hamper freedom so defined.

To be sure, only a few wealthy American egotists have both the arrogance and the means to live out untrammeled freedom to the full. But the virus of the idea is contagious, and it weakens the authority of the checks and balances that society needs if freedom is to be durable. Such unrestrained freedom—freedom that bows to no one and nothing outside itself and recognizes no external constraining standards—is disordered and deranged. Worse, it is nihilistic, in that there is absolutely *nothing* on the horizon—above, behind or around—to command the chooser's obedience or hamper the chooser's will.

To be fair, in the United States the will to power that is active in disordered freedom deals mostly in the small-souled currency of wealth, success and celebrity, and thus of human vanity. There is no power-hungry Caesar waiting to cross the Rubicon. Equally, America's nihilism of untrammeled freedom has so far been a soft and banal nihilism that flowers and fades harmlessly within the confines of the consumer paradise of the shopping mall, the online catalog and the video game. Besides, no one is fully consistent to his or her own philosophy, and there is always a long stretch of the downhill slope from the adolescent stage of soft nihilism to the delinquent and then to the decadent.

But such ideas in such a society will always have consequences, and when the causes of disordered freedom also spread to such vital spheres of American society as the government, the economy, law, education, medicine, science and technology, the consequences will at some point become lethal and unstoppable. The gap between the lightning and the thunder may be delayed, but such disordered freedom will one day prove disastrous when taken to the very end. It is literally irrational and irresponsible, for untrammeled freedom has no need to justify itself either by rational criteria or by any moral standard outside itself. It just *is*, an untrammeled will to power that is self-evident, self-justifying and self-destructive, and a mortal menace to the society that harbors it.

The conclusion for American freedom is inescapable. It is not enough to espouse freedom as the essence of America and to keep mouthing its matchless benefits. Freedom must be guarded vigilantly against internal as well as external dangers. However soft and however banal it is, unbounded freedom simply cannot restrain itself by itself, and in the end its self-destructive tendency will show through.

Put these three components together—the historical, the political and the moral—and the force of the paradox of freedom becomes clear. Neither law alone nor virtue alone can sustain freedom, because freedom always generates an abuse of power that endangers freedom. So law alone will override freedom by its very lack of self-restraint and by its inherent drive to compensate by replacing virtue with regulations. Virtue alone will always be too weak to sustain freedom, yet sometimes virtue alone will be too strong, in the sense that an excess of virtue can itself be an abuse of power. Thus, like any free people, Americans should never be naive and can never trust in freedom itself, for freedom alone cannot bear the weight of freedom. This is why freedom has a chronic habit of undermining and destroying itself. Again and again, more is less, and too much of a good thing becomes a bad thing in one of three ways:

When freedom runs to excess and breeds permissiveness and license.

When freedom so longs for its own security that its love of security undermines freedom ("The dangers of life are infinite," Goethe said, "and among them is safety").

When freedom becomes so caught up in its own glory that it justifies anything and everything done in its name, even such things as torture that contradict freedom.

Strikingly, the last decade has displayed clear examples of each of these corruptions writ large in American culture and in American foreign policy.

ALL ISSUES POINT TO FREEDOM

Third, sustainable freedom is urgent for America because many of the crises facing the United States have a direct bearing on freedom. The debt crisis is the most obvious. The question "What kind of a people do you think you are?" has been raised savagely by the grand financial crisis of 2008 and the recession that followed it. These two events were of world significance because they created the first global crisis in history that was caused principally by the United States, and they raise major questions for the republic. The first concerns the link between debt and freedom; the second concerns the mounting inequities between America's super-rich and everyone else; and the third concerns the place of money in national life when more and more of politics is "up for sale" and the United States resembles a plutocracy as much as a democracy.

The blunt fact is that America's grand promotion of debt-leveraged consumerism has stood Max Weber's famous thesis about the rise of capitalism on its head. It has scorned the early-American stress on hard work, savings, thrift and delayed gratification, and turned Americans into a nation of perpetual debtors who are now chided even by the Chinese and the Indians for their irresponsibility and "addiction to debt."[9]

America's fabled economic dominance has masked the fact of its dire financial indebtedness and therefore of the severe constraints on its real freedom. Few, if any, superpowers in history have been in deeper debt than the United States today. Whereas the British Empire in its heyday was the world's largest creditor, and Japan and China have that distinction today, the United States is both the world's dominant power and the world's largest debtor—with the debt going to finance consumption rather than infrastructure investment.

Thus, with the United States shifting from producing to consuming, with American citizens consuming more than they save and with the government spending more than it earns and promising to spend still more, America's household debt, government debt and international debt are all growing rapidly. Post–World War II America, it is said, has been driving forward on debtcraft, deficitry, and debtmanship.

The chickens are now coming home to roost, though so far most warnings have been dismissed as Chicken Little alarmism and the spending goes on. The George W. Bush administration, for example, financed the Iraq War through loans held by the Chinese rather than through taxes shouldered by the generation that declared the war. And the Obama administration has plunged the country even deeper still. Indeed, as many observed in light of the Iraq and Afghan wars, the tax cuts, the Wall Street bailouts, the stimulus packages and the new health care provisions, never has one generation spent so much of its children's wealth in such a short period and with so little to show for it.

But that was only the beginning of the Alice in Wonderland logic of the wider financial crisis. Huge gains on Wall Street kept going to individuals, while the huge losses went to the American public. Successes were well rewarded, and failures often went unpunished. Those who had been part of creating the problem were often the only ones deemed clever enough to remedy it.

"Happy is he who owes nothing," says a Roman proverb, for taking on too much debt is a rash bet against the future, the odds of which not even the Masters of the Universe can pretend to know. And needless to say, the deeper the debt, the less the freedom and flexibility. Some observers thought that this stark truth would prove the silver lining in the Wall Street crash of 2008 that would bring America to its senses. But did it? A huge spending tsunami had long been gathering speed and rolling fast toward shore. Then, compounded by the greed, hubris, dishonesty, myopia, corruption, careless lack of regulation and reckless folly of the housing bubble, the subprime derivatives and the crony capitalism of Wall Street and Washington, the crisis has shown the dire extent of American debt and the widespread bankruptcy of American trust and ethics in relation to free markets.

Much of America's financial strength is mortgaged to foreign investors, much is dependent on foreign sources of energy, and much is part of an exorbitant bill for health care, social security and the toxic subprime mortgages. During the Wall Street crisis, Warren Buffet was reported as saying, "You never know who is swimming naked until the tide goes out."[10] The current crisis mercilessly exposes the denuding of the American founders' wisdom about the need for leadership with character, freedom with virtue, business with integrity and trust, the rule of law with the cultivation of habits of the heart, education with an emphasis not only on grades and credentials but on the meaning of life, and medicine with human and ethical values as strong as the drives of science and technology.

CHALLENGES FROM
AROUND THE WORLD

Fourth, sustainable freedom is urgent for America because the recent global groundswell of disapproval of the United States has included very specific criticisms of American freedom. Each charge requires its own response, but Americans would be wise to consider the criticisms in light of the deeper issues to which they all point: the character and condition of freedom and the challenge of sustainable freedom as the founders understood it.

One criticism is that the current American vision of freedom is naive, with its blithe equation of freedom, democracy and free markets and its neglect of the cultural foundations necessary for them—or worse, that the Bush-era boasts of the New American Century were universalistic, messianic and utopian, with their dream of American-led democratic freedom ending tyranny on earth and ushering in peace among democratic nations.

Recent critics commonly cited four texts. One was the 1997 statement on behalf of the Project for the New American Century, because of the signers' later role in the policies of the George W. Bush administration. Another was "The National Security Strategy of the United States" presented to the Congress by the White House in September 2002, with its claim that there is "a single sustainable model for national success: freedom, democracy, and free enterprise."[11] The most important were the younger Bush's second inaugural address in January 2005 and his "State of the Union Address" a few weeks later. These offered a myriad of references to America's destiny in bringing freedom to the world, with "the ultimate goal of ending tyranny in our world."[12]

According to the critics, such celebrations of the American trinity—freedom, democracy and free markets—are more than the latest spasm of American exceptionalism, a passing neoconservative conceit or a misreading of America's "unipolar moment." They are a form of hubris and utopianism that is unwelcome in the world and disastrous for America. American-led, ever-unfolding freedom, widening democratic peace and never-ending prosperity are three of the last great expressions of the Enlightenment faith in a universal civilization—to be ushered in by the United States. America, Hegel wrote, is "the land of the future, where, in the ages that lie before us, the burden of the World's History shall reveal itself."[13]

The critics' charge is that this grandly inflated claim has become untethered from the prudence of the American founders, as well as from the Christian realism of earlier generations, not to speak of more recent realpolitik. It has the following effects.

It conflates America's uniqueness and her universality.

It forgets that nothing is more unexceptional than claims to exceptionalism. (Historians remind us that all of the world's seventy-odd empires have proclaimed it in their turn.[14])

It resembles the unfounded confidence in reason, freedom and progress of the ideologues of the French, Russian and Chinese revolutions. (George W. Bush's rhetoric was an eerie echo of the French revolutionary cry for a "universal crusade for liberty.")

It contradicts the American founders' clear preference for a republic rather than a democracy and for ordered liberty rather than mere freedom.

It ignores the fact that there are essential preconditions for freedom, different paths to freedom and different ways to be modern.

And it so underplays the place of irreducible conflict in the global era that it is rapidly becoming America's version of Kant's "perpetual peace" and Comte's "religion of humanity" all rolled into one.

In short, in the global era, George W. Bush's more exaggerated claims for freedom are a dangerous delusion that America cannot sustain and the world cannot afford.

TOO MUCH OF A GOOD THING

Another criticism from abroad is that American freedom is in danger of becoming too much of a good thing and that, as always, too much of a good thing is a bad thing. Claims to rights and entitlements without duty are destroying the cultural soil in which all rights and freedom itself have to be nourished; unregulated free markets are destroying America's social bonds; an excess of democracy is undermining the carefully crafted republic of the American founders; and an increasingly corrupt form of American freedom is causing a shift from constitutional liberalism to democratic illiberalism, and in the process damaging America itself.

In short, contrary to the founders—and in ways they do not realize themselves—Americans today are heedlessly pursuing a vision of freedom that is short-lived and suicidal. Once again, freedom without virtue, leadership without character, business without trust, law without customs, education without meaning and medicine, science and technology without human considerations can end only in disaster.

When exported abroad, the same rampant American freedom often undermines the traditional ways of life in other countries through its licentiousness, permissiveness and passion to transgress. Witness the vile inhumanity of American gangsta rap and the puerile antics of American stars such as Michael Jackson and starlets such as Britney Spears, Paris Hilton and Lindsay Lohan, and a nation's bizarre obsession with such decadence.

Thus the American Way, far from the last best hope for the world, is becoming a riot of indulgent freedom that is anything but positive and liberating. "License they mean when they cry liberty," John Milton warned in words that are widely echoed today.[15] After the younger Bush's second inaugural address, a Middle Eastern leader said to a friend of mine, "Every time the president says freedom, I see license."

One last criticism is that American freedom has simply become an ideology—a set of high-sounding ideas used as spiritual weapons for America's real interests, such as maintaining dominance or protecting America's ravenous need for resources such as oil. Freedom, in other words, is the shield behind which America uses force in yet another attempt to remake the world in its own image—or as it imagines itself to be. ("With God's help," U.S. Senator Kenneth Wherry declared of Chiang Kai-shek's China in the 1940s, "we will lift Shanghai up and up until it is just like Kansas City."[16])

Freedom, after all, has already been used to accompany and justify many of the darkest stains in America's history, starting with the evils of slavery and the near-genocide of Native Americans and reaching down to Guantanamo Bay and Abu Ghraib.

CRISIS OF CULTURAL AUTHORITY

Put these four points together—and they highlight the significance of the present crisis of freedom. At the very least they demonstrate the danger of complacent inattention to the character of freedom and in particular to the indispensable notion of sustainable freedom that is the key to the founders' design of the American experiment.

More seriously still, these four points add up to the fact that freedom has become America's Achilles' heel, and the American republic is undergoing a profound crisis that has been variously described as a crisis of faith, a legitimation crisis, a crisis of civilizational morale and a crisis of cultural authority. The center no longer holds; the core has lost its compelling power; the moral and social ecology of the nation has been contaminated; the different spheres of society are undermining each other; and the escalation of the extremes is underway.

There is a straightforward reason why the United States is vulnerable to such a crisis of cultural authority. As the world's first new nation, America is distinctively a nation by intention and by ideas. Unlike most other nations, the core beliefs that make up American identity and character do not trail off into the mists of antiquity, and they are not the product of centuries-old habits of the heart. Taking off from their sturdy seventeenth-century beginnings, they arose in a sunburst of brilliant thinking and daring institution-building by a generation whose vision charted the course of America's meteoric rise to greatness. Yet the very clarity and centrality of those beliefs create unique problems for the United States when they are called into question, as they have been recently.

In the 1960s, the student protests in particular and the counterculture as a whole represented an earlier expression of the crisis of cultural authority. Today's crisis of cultural authority is far deeper, though the movements expressing it in public are far weaker. The Tea Party movement is the carrier on the right and the Occupy Wall Street movement is the carrier on the left.

In terms of style, these two movements are similar. Each owes much to the hi-tech advances of the Internet era, which they also share with the highly diverse movements that in early 2011 made up the "Arab Spring"—for example, in their common use of SADNs (self-assembled dynamic networks) to link their adherents and promote their causes in public.

In terms of substance, however, the two American movements could not appear more different. The Tea Partyers on the right are protesting the crisis of dysfunctional republicanism, citing the bloated growth of unchecked statism and lamenting such dire crises as the profligacy of debt spending. The Occupy Wall Streeters on the left are protesting the crisis of dysfunctional democracy, citing the savage inequities between the super-rich "1 percenters" and the rest—the "99 percenters"—and lamenting the heartless face of economic reductionism and unfettered capitalism and their consequences for the poor and for the earth.

Republicanism, democracy and capitalism—apart from the faith communities, there are no institutions whose character and crises are so foundational and decisive for America. Seen this way, the very different concerns of the two movements are in fact closer than many people realize, for knowingly or not, each addresses a key aspect of the crisis of cultural authority that must be resolved if the democratic republic of the United States is to thrive again.

In its stand for classical republican freedom, the Tea Party movement stems from the fact that America is becoming a mere superstate and is therefore increasingly a republic in name only. In the lives of most Americans, the founders' notion of sustainable freedom has all but disappeared. And in its stand for classical democratic justice, the Occupy Wall Street movement stems from the fact that America is becoming a moneyed oligarchy and is therefore increasingly a democracy in name only. In election after election, the voices of money and special interests outweigh the voice of the people.

To be sure, neither movement is at present doing justice to the core crisis of cultural authority that lies deeper than their publicly stated concerns. And sadly for each movement, the noisy manner in which they make their case, not to speak of the distorted ways they are reported, alienates the wider public rather than illuminating their central point. This frustrates rather than furthers the communication of their legitimate concerns. The crisis is there all the same, and serious national discussion must engage the issues raised by both movements. But the debate must also go deeper and show how their respective issues can be resolved only in a broader understanding of the character and crisis of the great American experiment.

Should this not happen, the evident shortcomings of the two movements, like the flaws of the "Arab Spring" and the 60s counterculture before them, will block their potential and condemn them to end closer to the disappointments that flowed from the revolution of 1789 than to the achievements of the revolution of 1776.

Whatever the outcome, it is beyond dispute that two and a third centuries after the audacious work of the founding fathers, with all the changes and developments that have occurred since then, a full range of questions is pressing for America's attention. These questions call for an American Cicero to stand against the weakening of the republic or for leaders of the stature of Abraham Lincoln and Franklin Roosevelt to wrestle with the stakes for democracy and international leadership, and so point the way to a renewal that could be a "new birth of freedom" today.

The truth is that, as the saying carved in granite on the Korean War Memorial in Washington, D.C., declares, "Freedom is not free." This means not only that blood is the price of defending freedom abroad, but also that, if freedom is to flourish and endure, freedom's essential character and conditions must be guarded vigilantly, both at home and overseas. Freedom can no more take a holiday from history than from gravity, and the plain fact is that it is harder to be free than not to be free, for freedom's fire has not only to be lit once but must be kindled and rekindled all over again in each succeeding generation. How else are we to understand the fact that freedom never lasts and that freedom always becomes the greatest enemy to freedom?

Hubris is not simply arrogance but presumption born of the illusion of invulnerability. That is why nations at the height of their power and prosperity are especially deaf to warnings. But what an irony if the descendants of the American founders, who dared to think that a free people could become free, live free and for all time remain free, should abandon their founders' provisions and condemn America to be one of the shorter-lived great powers in history—a world empire measured in decades rather than centuries.

STAR-SPANGLED IRONY

This, then, is the theme of this book: the present crisis of America's ordered liberty and sustainable freedom. What we are witnessing is a gathering crisis of freedom, stemming from a dangerous neglect of the notion of ordered liberty that alone allows a democracy to be durable and a free people to stay free. The founders gave no name to their vision of sustainable freedom; Tocqueville called it "the habits of the heart," and for reasons we shall see, I call it "the golden triangle of freedom."

If the founders were correct, contemporary America's pursuit of political leadership without character, economic enterprise without ethics and trust, scientific progress without human values, freedom without virtue and negative freedom without positive freedom can end only in disaster. It rings the death knell of sustainable freedom, and as it works itself out socially and politically in countless areas, it makes the decline of America only a matter of time.

To be sure, *sustainability* is a recent and even voguish term, though the history of human civilizations shows that the challenge long precedes the word. The unchanging imperative of every political order is to continue to be, though not a single civilization in all of human history has so far developed immunity to the forces of decline.

Yet the irony is that Americans, whose founders addressed the issue as shrewdly as anyone in history, now pay scant attention to their founders or to the sustainable freedom that underlies their strength and prosperity.

And Americans indulge this neglect at the very moment when they can least afford to—the moment that spells out the blunt alternative: renewal or decline.

A sustainable society is a self-renewing society in which, from generation to generation, the citizens choose to do what the society needs them to do if it is to last—in other words, a society in which leaders and citizens alike have cultivated the habits of the heart to do without thinking what they need to do if they were to think about it. That is not happening in America today with freedom.

There are isolated voices that raise the issue—for example, John Gardner, in his 1963 book *Self-Renewal*: "Suppose one tried to imagine a society that would be relatively immune to decay—an ever-renewing society. What would it be like? What would be the ingredients that provide the immunity?"[17] He even proposed a Department of Continuous Renewal.

But such voices are rare, and such questions are rarely raised today. The result is a star-spangled irony. Americans today speak endlessly about sustainable growth, sustainable development, a sustainable future and the "conservation" or "ecology" of this, that and the other. And after the Minneapolis bridge collapse in 2007, they talk of the threat of the decaying infrastructure that supports America's aging roads and bridges. But amazingly few pay serious attention to notions such as sustainable freedom, the ecology and conservation of liberty, the infrastructure of America's foundations of freedom—or to the idea that freedom itself requires a living system of immunity if it is to stay healthy. This carelessness may prove lethal.

LIVE FREE FOR ALL TIME OR DIE BY OUR OWN HAND

I write as a visitor to America, but one who is a long-time admirer of the United States—though even that is suspect to some Americans. Some view an outsider's admiration as support for American cultural imperialism, while others suspect that fulsome compliments are simply a dose of syrup to prepare for another intemperate bout of anti-Americanism. On both accounts, quite the contrary.

It is a mark of healthy societies that, in times of change and crisis, they throw up leaders worthy of the hour. At this point, the United States urgently requires such a leader to lead and the nation to follow.

But it is also plain that recent American presidents, entrusted with delivering the State of the Union, have been either unable or unwilling to address these particular issues—in the elder Bush's case, out of discomfort with "the vision thing"; in Bill Clinton's, being mired in scandal; in the younger Bush's, being preoccupied with terrorism and national security; and in Barack Obama's, being buffeted with global problems as no president before him.

Yet if the founders of the republic were correct, the ultimate challenge facing America will always be the enemy within—domestic rather than international. Intercontinental ballistic missiles, dirty bombs, cyber-security and the ferocities of terrorism notwithstanding, the deepest menace will not come from abroad but home. Many people quote Arnold Toynbee's repeated observation, "History shows that all great nations commit suicide."[18] But the theme of this book owes far more to Abraham Lincoln's expressly American understanding of the challenge: "If destruction be our lot, we must ourselves be its author and finisher. As a nation of freemen, we must live through all time, or die by suicide."[19]

No one who knows the classics well would be shocked by such bluntness, though many Americans today would be. Some people talk of the "loss" of freedom as if citizens mislaid it in a fit of absentmindedness. Others talk of the "miscarriage" of freedom as if the loss was unfortunate but caused by factors outside their control. I have even heard people talk of the "aborting" of freedom, as if someone could be rid of freedom but the ridder remains alive and well. To be sure, Americans have become some of history's grand masters of casual abortion, but that metaphor does not come close to the truth of what is happening with freedom. Lincoln was right: the precise term is *suicide*.

The free people of the American republic, who also happen to be citizens of the modern world's sole superpower, have no one to blame and nothing to fear but themselves. There is no question about the earlier menace of the Nazis and Communists, and now Islamic extremists, but in the end the ultimate threat to the American republic will be Americans. The problem is not wolves at the door but termites in the floor. Powerful free people die only by their own hand, and free people have no one to blame but themselves. What the world seems fascinated to watch but powerless to stop is the spectacle of a free people's suicide.

Not surprisingly, Americans are currently touchy about outside comments, and any criticism is apt to be heard as anti-American. Yet however long the odds and thankless the task, addressing the future of the world's lead society in a global era is too important to be left to its own citizens alone. America has long prided itself on being a "nation of nations." But though America is made up of peoples from all around the world, America's perspectives are often maddeningly parochial and sometimes give the impression of American autism.

This paradox needs to be overcome, not just so that America may listen to the world, but also so that the world may learn from the best of America. For one of the great ironies of our time is that just when the American experiment is more relevant to the world than ever before, America is in danger of alienating the world and cutting herself off from the source of her own greatness.

For all the vaunted parallels, the United States is not Rome, and she will not "fall" with twenty-first-century Visigoths rampaging down Pennsylvania Avenue. That is to confuse the "fall" of the Roman republic with the fall of the Roman Empire and to fail to recognize how Americans themselves are already the destroying vandals of their own heritage.

Nor is the United States Europe, and Americans will not follow the European path. But just as the collapse of European civilization was so cruelly exposed in the two World Wars and long prefigured in the warnings of Jacob Burckhardt and others, so America's writing on the wall is evident to those who are watching now. Nearly a hundred years ago, the world's last great empire, from whom Americans won their freedom and whom they have succeeded, was almost undone through a foolish policy of appeasement ("peace, peace, when there was no peace"). America's problem today is different but equally perilous: a general complacency bred of long prosperity and recent supremacy in world affairs ("All is well, all is well, when all is not well"). It is time to wake again.

THE ROAD MAP
AND THE CHALLENGE

My approach will be simple and straightforward:

In the second chapter, I will examine the founders' understanding of the three essential tasks they were addressing in the "great experiment" in freedom that the American Revolution began, and I will underscore how the current generation has neglected the third task—the all-important one today.

In the third chapter, I will contrast these challenges with the founders' realism about the classical understanding of why no political systems ever endured; how they attempted—daringly—to use history to defy history; and how most Americans today have no knowledge or interest in any of these things.

In the fourth chapter, we will explore the founders' solution to the challenge of sustaining freedom as well as the irony that, if there were those in their generation who mistakenly thought that the republic could be sustained by virtue alone, there are many today who make the equal and opposite mistake: thinking that republican freedom can be sustained without any virtue at all and exercised without any restraint.

In the fifth chapter, we will examine the domestic condition of American freedom today by looking at the present culture wars as a second American freedom war with decisive implications for America's future.

In the sixth chapter, we will do the same for America's international standing by looking at responses to recent foreign policy in light of the question "Is America's superpower influence an empire worthy of free people?"

And in the seventh and last chapter, we will examine the grounds for a possible American restoration and then finish with a reflection on the essence of America that is symbolized by the American eagle and its implications for the present generation's choice between decline and renewal.

Are there enough citizens who are still able to turn aside from the tyranny of the "obsessive now" and consider a restoration of the first things of this great republic? Only God knows. Would it be a demanding task? Yes. But insurmountable? No. Better that Americans consider their peril in good time than sleep on until it is too late. I write with urgency, but also with hope for the outcome of this crisis that matches my high esteem for Americans and for the historic accomplishment of this great country.

Once again, the challenge is plain. This is another "age of trial," as John Adams said of the period leading up to the revolution. If World War II ushered in the "American Century," as Henry Luce pronounced famously in 1941, the United States is now toward the climax of a generation-long crisis of cultural authority that is "the American hour"—a time of crucial opportunity and challenge that will be decisive for the coming century.

This is both America's peril and promise. The peril lies in the fact that the present is a time of reckoning that gathers up issues and controversies of the last generation whose resolution can be delayed no longer. The promise lies in the fact that the present moment invites all Americans to consider what it means today to "let America be America" and thus to live up to the still unfulfilled potential of America's great experiment in freedom.

"What kind of a people do you think you are?" America's only way forward lies down the path of tackling and resolving this major issue: how can a free republic maintain its freedom? The future of America and the future of the world in the global era await America's answer to this question. Those who aspire to be like Rome in their beginnings must avoid being like Rome at their ending. Rome and its republic fell and so too will the American republic—unless . . .

2

Always Free, Free Always

In 1843, a twenty-one-year-old Massachusetts scholar was doing research on the American Revolution and what led up to it. Among those he interviewed was Captain Levi Preston, a Yankee who was seventy years his senior and had fought at both Lexington and Concord.

"Captain Preston," the young man began, "what made you go to the Concord Fight on April 19, 1775?"

"What did I go for?" The old soldier, every bit his ninety-one years, was very bowed, so he raised himself to his full height, taken aback that anyone should ask a question about anything so obvious.

The young man tried again. "Yes, my histories tell me that you men of the Revolution took up arms against 'intolerable oppressions.' What were they?"

"Oppressions? I didn't feel them."

"What, you were not oppressed by the Stamp Act?"

"I never saw one of those stamps," Captain Preston replied. "I certainly never paid a penny for them."

"Well, what about the tea tax?"

"Tea tax? I never drank a drop of the stuff," the old veteran replied. "The boys threw it all overboard."

"Then I suppose you had been reading Harrington, or Sidney and Locke about the eternal principles of liberty?"

"Never heard of 'em," Captain Preston said. "We read only the Bible, the Catechism, Watts's *Psalms and Hymns* and the Almanac."

"Well then, what was the matter? And what did you mean in going to the fight?"

"Young man," Captain Preston stated firmly, "what we meant in going for those Redcoats was this: We always had been free, and we meant to be free always. They didn't mean we should."[1]

Always free, free always—the magnificent daring of that thought deserves thought. For one thing, it speaks volumes about the freedom that was the passion and goal of the revolution. As historian David Hackett Fischer points out, it also shows clearly that Captain Preston's sense of freedom, a freedom for which he would live and die, was not something that can be understood only by studying great declarations, such as the Magna Carta and the Declaration of Independence, or great ideas and books, such as the writings of John Locke and Edmund Burke. In Alexander Hamilton's words, "The sacred rights of mankind are not to be rummaged for among old parchments or dusty records. They are written, as with a sunbeam, in the whole volume of human nature, by the hand of the Divinity itself."[2]

In the term that Tocqueville made famous later, freedom for Captain Preston and countless more like him was a habit of the heart, and it was kept strong by symbols and icons such as the Liberty Tree, the Liberty Bell and later the Stars and Stripes and the Statue of Liberty, rather than simply by books and declarations. As freeborn Englishmen, the colonists saw freedom as their birthright and as natural as their mother's milk and the New England air they breathed—even if they had to contend for it against their mother country. When Tocqueville witnessed a Fourth of July celebration in Albany, New York, in 1831, he observed, "It seemed that an electric current made the hearts vibrate."[3]

Even more extraordinarily, Captain Preston, along with the leaders of the revolution and many others in his generation, clearly believed that freedom could last forever. The realism that is more normal to human experience was stated bluntly by Machiavelli: "It is impossible to order a perpetual republic."[4] Yet only a century later and more than a century before the American Revolution, Hobbes spoke of building a country "as immortal, or long-lived, as the world."[5] And James Harrington, in his fictional *Oceana*, had written of a republic that was an "immortal commonwealth."[6]

But that was literature and those were words. The revolution's project was the real world. Nothing—absolutely nothing—in the entire American experiment is more daring than this, the conviction that a free people can *become free, live free and remain free*. They can be free forever.

But can freedom truly last forever? Americans in this generation may take freedom for granted, glorying in how they have become free and basking in how they enjoy freedom today. But they need to see that their nation's superpower status creates the illusion of invulnerability that is the core of hubris. Of all times, times of dominance are the most dangerous in which to be complacent about freedom, for in the life cycle of great powers only one thing finally follows dominance: decline. Dominance eventually leads to decline as surely as day ends in night. Thus dominance is precisely the time to think through whether a free people can remain free forever, why the founding generation dared to believe in such a history-defying feat and what the present generation is doing today to ensure that they play their part in this magnificent venture.

There are three tasks in establishing a free society that hopes to remain free—winning freedom, ordering freedom and sustaining freedom—and each was a prominent consideration to the American founders. Yet such a simple statement is beguiling, and masks a myriad of deeper issues, beginning with the sad fact that as time goes by, free people take freedom more and more for granted. Then, as they progress from the first task to the second and third, they increasingly relax, even though the last task raises the stiffest challenge of all, a challenge that stares every generation of free people in the eye: Are we sustaining the freedom of which we are fortunate to be heirs?

WINNING FREEDOM

The first task, *winning freedom*, is understandably considered the noblest and most glorious of the three, and it easily overshadows the others. As such, it becomes enshrined as the core of a nation's identity and its founding myth, and is passed down from generation to generation and celebrated in a thousand stories, symbols and toasts. In this sense Americans celebrate 1776 as the English celebrated the Glorious Revolution of 1688, as the French 1789, the Russians 1917 and the Chinese 1949. In each case, a revolutionary party, fighting in the name of freedom, overthrew some form of an *ancien regime* or foreign control and successfully declared independence.

No country celebrates its revolution like the United States and feels closer to its spirit. Winning freedom is the glory of the American Revolution, of the Declaration of Independence and of the War of Independence—and of 1776 and July 4 (though the date should really be July 2, the actual day when the Continental Congress voted to "dissolve the connection" with Great Britain). Americans will therefore always thrill to the recounting of how "the glorious cause of America" was won, of how a small, ill-equipped and untrained band of freedom-loving patriots prevailed against the most formidable force sent out by the most formidable empire of their day.

Lasting more than eight years, the Revolutionary War was second only to the Vietnam War in length, though now eclipsed by Iraq and Afghanistan. And with twenty-five thousand killed, it was proportionately one of the bloodiest of all American wars. But it was victorious. "The British were completely disgraced," the *New York Consti-*

tutional Gazette trumpeted after George Washington's success at Boston in 1776. "Free men under arms had triumphed, with all the world watching."[7] The "Sons of Liberty" had proved that they were neither "summer soldiers" nor "sunshine patriots." They had pledged their "lives, their fortunes, and their sacred honor," and had won the day and secured their cause: freedom.

In countless speeches, the point is made rightly that nothing is more powerful than free men fighting for their freedom and defending their own land and homes. As General Washington declared to the Continental Army, "Remember officers and soldiers that you are free men fighting for the blessings of liberty." Or again, "Remember . . . what a few brave men contending in their own land, and in the best of causes can do, against base hirelings and mercenaries."[8] As if to support the point, the Hessian officers hired by George III as mercenaries were heard to remark that they had never considered it their duty to inquire which of the two sides in the American controversy was right. They were simply doing their job.

This truth highlights a key feature of how America won freedom. Lexington and Concord were not the storming of the Bastille or of the Winter Palace in St. Petersburg. Nor was the Revolutionary War like the Long March of Mao Tse-tung. Unlike the French, Russian and Chinese, who all fought for freedom from a position of abject oppression and tyranny, the American colonists fought for freedom as some of the freest and most prosperous people of their time.

The American revolutionaries were born in freedom, schooled in freedom and fought for a heritage of freedom they had grown to know as theirs. In Lord Acton's summary, "No people was so free as the insurgents; no government less oppressive than the government which they overthrew."[9] After all, in Montesquieu's famous compliment, the English loved liberty "prodigiously," and England was unique for having political liberty as its animating principle, so that it was really "a republic concealed under the form of a monarchy."[10] As Madison put it in praise of Montesquieu, he saw the constitution

of England as the very "mirrour of political liberty."[11] Jean Jacques
Rousseau had also acknowledged that the English were "nearer to
liberty than all the others."[12]

When Tocqueville visited Harvard in 1831, Joseph Quincy, the
president, asserted that Massachusetts was almost as free before the
revolution as she was in their time: "We put the name of the people
where formerly was that of the king. Otherwise nothing changed
among us."[13] Edmund Burke underscored the point in his famous
"Speech on Conciliation with America" in 1775. The prime feature of
Americans, he warned Parliament, is "a love of freedom." Indeed,
"this fierce spirit of liberty is stronger in the English colonies probably
than in any other people of the earth." And why? They are the descendants of Englishmen. "They are therefore not only devoted to
liberty, but to liberty according to English ideas, and on English
principles."[14]

Two centuries later, Winston Churchill was equally forceful on a
visit to Williamsburg, Virginia, when he was asked what he felt about
a city that played such a role in "the revolutionary war against the
English." The prime minister snorted, "Revolution against the
English! Nay, it was a reaffirmation of English rights. Englishmen
battling a Hun king and his Hessian hirelings to protect their English
birthright." Or as he said on a more formal occasion, "The Declaration of Independence is not only an American document. It follows
on the Magna Carta and the Bill of Rights as the third great title-
deed in which the liberties of the English-speaking people are
founded."[15]

Saying this does not diminish the achievement of the American
Revolution. In the words of George Trevelyan, an eminent historian
on the defeated side, "It may be doubted whether so small a number
of men ever employed so short a space of time with greater and more
lasting effects upon the history of the world."[16] The revolutionaries'
winning freedom was and always will be a glorious achievement, and
gloriously built upon. But it is still true that in winning freedom,

they went from freedom to *greater freedom*. The rhetoric of "slavery" and "bondage" was sincere but relative. As Captain Preston acknowledged, he had felt no "oppressions." He and his compatriots were free men fighting for even greater freedom from the "oppression" of what was perhaps the freest nation of their time; much of the world spoke admiringly of "English liberty."

ORDERING FREEDOM

Such is the success and glory of the first task of the revolution that it will always overshadow the second: *ordering freedom*. Yet the second task was no less daring and significant. In pulling down what are seen as the oppressive structures and practices of the old regime, successful revolutions inevitably create a vacuum into which can flow a hundred forces lethal to the ideals for which the revolution was fought. Revolutions may exorcise a haunted house, only to open the door to seven demons worse than the first.

The French, Russian and Chinese revolutions are cautionary examples of this truth. Far from ordering freedom—or equality, fraternity, a classless society or any of the shining visions for which they fought—they spiraled down to demonic disorder and tyranny—often far worse than any evil they replaced.

Flogging the dead horse of communism is all too easy, but the baleful shadow of 1789 still lingers over part of our world today. What the French did, in Lord Acton's view, was to copy the American idea of revolution but not the American idea of government. Where once they had an absolute monarch, they enthroned in his place an absolute people whose unchecked appetite for power became voracious and destructive.

The result was an authoritarian democracy and a hunger for glory that led easily to dictatorship. ("They must have glory, the satisfaction of vanity," Napoleon declared as he ended the republic. "But as for liberty, they understand nothing about it."[17]) Until the French reign of terror under Citizen Robespierre was superseded by the Nazi death camps in the twentieth century, it was widely considered the epitome of European evil, a flagrant betrayal of "*Liberté, Egalité, Fraternité*" and a terrible premonition of modern evils to come. What was horrendous was not only the Terror in Paris itself, when the workings of the kangaroo courts became grotesque and the jaws of the guillotine were insatiable, but the horror of the "Franco-French wars" in which Frenchmen fought Frenchmen and the barbarity of the new secularist state far eclipsed the much-cited religious evils of the Inquisition and the St. Bartholomew's Day massacre. In their pitiless extermination of a quarter of a million people—a third of the population of the Vendee in 1793—the Jacobins and their genocide-before-the-term-genocide prefigured such twentieth-century horrors as Stalin's terror famine in the Ukraine, Mao Tse-tung's cultural revolution and Pol Pot's killing fields in Cambodia. Equally, their chilling justifications for mass murder used logic and language that was echoed almost exactly by Hitler and Himmler.

Perceptive as ever, the great Irish political leader and philosopher Edmund Burke saw the end of the French Revolution from the beginning and cut to the core of the problem at once. In his first reaction to the news of its outbreak, he wrote to a friend:

> The spirit is impossible not to admire; but the old Parisian ferocity has broken out in a shocking manner. It is true that this may be no more than a sudden explosion: If so no indication can be taken from it. But if it should be character rather than accident, then that people are not fit for Liberty, and must have a Strong hand like that of their former managers to coerce them. Men must have a certain fund of natural moderation to qualify them for Freedom, else it becomes noxious to themselves and a perfect Nuisance to everybody else. . . . To form a solid constitution requires Wisdom as well as spirit, and whether the French have wise heads among them, or if they

possess such whether they have authority equal to their wisdom, is to be seen.[18]

Washington, Adams, Hamilton, the early Madison and other American leaders were all distinctively different from the French revolutionaries. With exceptions such as Jefferson and Paine, most of the American founders saw their revolution in marked contrast to that of the French. Not only did they win freedom, they also ordered it. Having won freedom, they went on to provide a moral, cultural and, above all, political framework in which freedom could flourish. People who would be free must be able to rule themselves, which is another way of saying that free people need saving from themselves as much as from an oppressive regime. In the famous picture of Cicero, a well-ordered state is like a harmonious song—anything but an improvisation.

If 1776 and the revolution are shorthand for winning freedom, then 1787 and the Constitution are the shorthand for ordering freedom. The result is a republic rather than a democracy and constitutional liberalism rather than pure liberalism. According to such a view, an unordered or excessive democracy may well undermine republican freedom. "We are in bondage to the law," Cicero declared, "in order that we might be free."[19] Freedom requires peace, and peace requires personal as well as social order. In Santayana's words about the second, "In order to be truly and happily free you must be safe."[20]

The natural tendency here is to rhapsodize about the achievement of the Constitution and the brilliance of *The Federalist*, which is its best interpreter, and then to stop at that. Prime Minister Gladstone described the former as "the most wonderful work ever struck off at a given time by the brain and purpose of man," and Jefferson described the brilliant arguments on behalf of the Constitution as "the best commentary on the principles of government which ever was written."[21]

The Constitution was indeed a unique masterpiece of political design, but it was also more than that. Madison admitted that it was not a "faultless" work. And commenting on its failure to deal adequately with religious liberty, with states rights and above all with the evil of slavery, Lord Acton's summary was markedly different from Gladstone's: "Slavery was deplored, was denounced, and was retained. . . . Weighed in the scales of Liberalism, the instrument as it stood was a monstrous fraud."[22] Yet such deep inconsistencies aside, the founders' writings prove that their notion of ordered freedom and "tempered liberty" went far beyond the foundational articles of law passed in Philadelphia in 1787 and the Bill of Rights in 1791. It included an understanding of the cultural foundations needed to foster freedom (the subject of chapter 4) as well as of the individual character of leaders best suited to lead free people and not lapse into despotism or slide toward corruption.

Why this stress on ordered liberty? On the one hand, America's Puritan heritage, derived from the Hebrew Scriptures, taught most early Americans that the Constitution was more than laws, however fundamental and clear. In its essence, the roots of the United States Constitution can be traced back to the notion of covenant from the Jewish Torah. Through its rediscovery in the Protestant Reformation, the idea of covenant had touched such countries as Switzerland, Scotland and Germany; and through the Puritans, it had shaped New England churches, then marriages, then townships, then colonies and finally the new nation itself.

For the Jewish people, a covenant could and would always be broken and could always degenerate into the oppressive legalism and barren ritualism against which the prophets thundered. But it was still always more than law. The covenant was a mutually binding commitment by a group of freely consenting partners that set out a way of life rather than a matter of mere law and a way of life that was to lead to a just, free, peaceful and healthy commonwealth—in a word, to *shalom*, or human flourishing. So also did the constitutional provisions for freedom in 1787. Sworn to with the same free consent and with the same binding commitment, they were designed to create "a more perfect union," a framework within which free citizens could live freely and peacefully—each "under his own vine," as Washington expressed it in a direct echo of the Hebrew prophet Micah.

More to the point, the provisions and protections of the Constitution were not set up as a professional preserve for scholars, lawyers and activists. Nor were they to be cordoned off for courts and judges alone. They were the very provisions by which "We the people" constituted themselves a union, and therefore they were to be cultivated and guarded by those whose stake in it was strongest and whom it benefited most: families, churches, synagogues, schools, communities and the citizenry at large. In Lord Acton's words, "In obeying laws to which all men have agreed, all men, in reality, govern themselves."[23]

On the other hand, all these influences behind the Constitution—which also included the civic republicanism of the classical world and the emphasis on "moral sense" of the British Enlightenment—came to be held increasingly in conscious tension with ideas from the French Revolution. Earlier, Thomas Jefferson was an enthusiastic apologist for the twin ideas that the French Revolution was the continuation and fulfillment of the American Revolution and that the French Revolution was the happy child of the French Enlightenment.

Both these beliefs were dealt a terrible blow by the course of events in France, which culminated in the execution of the king and queen and in the reign of terror that followed. As the French Revolution became godless, bloodthirsty and tyrannical, disentanglement from the ruins of collapsed hopes in France showed ever more clearly the wisdom of ordered American freedom.

Jefferson, like Charles James Fox in England, was one of the last to appreciate that the French Revolution's inability to order freedom carried the seeds of its own disaster. As late as April 1791, Fox hailed the new French constitution giddily as "the most glorious and stupendous edifice of liberty, which had been erected on the foundation of human liberty in any time or century."[24] Jefferson took his side against Burke with equal passion, and in a foretaste of postmodern debunking, ascribed "wicked motives" to Burke's "mask of virtue and patriotism."[25]

Yet Burke was right and Jefferson wrong. On the one hand, this naivety made Jefferson a poor analyst of what was actually happening in the course of the French Revolution, even when he was living in Paris. After the fall of the Bastille in July 1789, he wrote to Thomas Paine from the French capital, "Tranquility is well established in Paris, and tolerably so throughout the whole kingdom; and I think there is no possibility now of anything hindering their final establishment of a good constitution, which will in its principles and merit be between that of England and the United States."[26]

On the other hand, Jefferson's romance with France and his intense dislike of England made him remarkably cavalier in condoning the revolutionary violence of the French. In words that terrorists from the Jacobins to the Irish Republican Army to Timothy McVeigh have invoked ever since—which may again come to haunt America in the future if picked up and acted on by the American militia—Jefferson wrote to Abigail Adams after Shay's rebellion, "What signify a few lives lost in a century or two? The tree of liberty must be refreshed from time to time with the blood of patriots and tyrants. It is its natural manure."[27]

Later Jefferson wrote even more extravagantly to William Short, his private secretary, about the execution of Louis XVI ("the expunging of that officer"). The logic of his words has rightly been described as closer to Stalin, Mao Tse-tung and Pol Pot than to Washington, Hamilton and Burke.

The liberty of the whole earth was depending on the issue of the contest, and was ever such a prize won with so little innocent blood? My own affections have been deeply wounded by some of the martyrs to this cause, but rather than it should have failed, I would have seen half the earth desolated. Were there but an Adam and an Eve left in every country, and left free, it would be better than as it is now.[28]

Luckily for Jefferson, the French Revolution died the year before he ran for president. "Citizens," Napoleon declared bluntly, "the Revolution is established upon the principles which began it: it is ended."[29] By then Jefferson had foresworn the extravagance of his earlier views, and with a politician's consummate gall he then blamed the confusion of "the cause of France with that of freedom" on his Federalist enemies. But to the end, he called himself "a sincere well-wisher to the success of the French revolution," and the reason for his hopes was revealing: that "it may end in the establishment of a free & well-ordered republic."[30]

Jefferson's pious wish for a well-ordered republic in France had been the prime concern for Washington, Adams, Madison, Hamilton and Burke for the United States from the beginning. As Burke wrote in his *Reflections on the Revolution in France,*

> When I see the spirit of liberty in action, I see a strong principle at work; and this, for a while, is all I can know of it. The wild gas, the fixed air is plainly broke loose: but we ought to suspend our judgment until the first effervescence is a little subsided, till the liquor is cleared, and until we see something deeper than the agitation of troubled and frothy surface. . . . The effect of liberty to individuals is, that they may do what they please: We ought to see what it will please them to do, before we risque congratulations, which may soon be turned into complaints.[31]

What was decisive for a revolution on behalf of freedom, Burke wrote in words that the American framers spent their lives exemplifying, was to see how liberty had been "combined with government" and with other institutions and values such as morality, religion, civil and social manners. The wild gas of liberty was one thing. A well-ordered free republic with a clear separation and delineation of powers was another. In our day, when weak or failing states pose as great a threat to freedom as tyranny, the point must never be forgotten: order without freedom may be a manacle, but freedom without order is a mirage.

SUSTAINING FREEDOM

The third task of establishing a free republic is both the hardest and the least discussed today: *sustaining freedom*. This is perhaps surprising because, as Montesquieu noted, "states have the same object in general, which is to maintain themselves."[32] Often the sole nod to the place this occupied in the thinking of the founders is a passing reference to Benjamin Franklin's celebrated words as he came out of the Constitutional Convention in Philadelphia and its four months of secret deliberations. Asked by a certain Mrs. Powel what kind of government they had bestowed on the country, he replied, "A republic, Madam—if you can keep it."[33]

The revolutionaries had won freedom. Then they had ordered the freedom they had won. But freedom was still not ensured. The challenge from then on was to sustain freedom—almost a dare, most certainly a duty, and one that is fraught with many dangers. As Thomas Paine wrote, "Those who expect to reap the blessings of freedom must, like men, undergo the fatigues of supporting it."[34]

Needless to say, Franklin's and Paine's voices were not alone at the time. The magnificent simplicity of Captain Preston's "always free, free always" could be matched by others in the Revolutionary War— for example, General Nathaniel Greene in his impassioned letter to Samuel Ward as the colonies shifted from fighting for freedom to fighting for "independency":

Heaven hath decreed that tottering empire Britain to irretrievable ruin and thanks to God, since Providence hath so determined, America must raise an empire of permanent duration, supported upon the grand pillars of Truth, Freedom, and Religion, encouraged by the smiles of Justice and supported by her own patriotic sons.[35]

Burke argued to the English that, like property, liberty was a "patrimony" and a "pedigree of rights" handed down from generation to generation, a legacy that was always in need of transmission and always capable of improvement: "The people of England well know that the idea of inheritance furnishes a sure principle of conservation and a sure principle of transmission, without at all excluding a principle of improvement."[36]

James Madison's final "advice to my country" was that above all "the Union of the States be cherished and perpetuated."[37] More than fifty years after the revolution, a twenty-eight-year-old Abraham Lincoln was invited to address the Young Men's Lyceum in Springfield, Illinois. He took as his topic for the evening "The Perpetuation of our Political Institutions"—a remarkable testimony both to Lincoln and to the continuing power of this concern to assess our "account running" half a century after the revolutionary generation—in order to keep it running.

Far from a fleeting thought, this theme became stronger still when Lincoln ran for the presidency as the Civil War loomed. In his address to the Agricultural Society in Milwaukee, Wisconsin, on September 30, 1859, he finished with the story of the ancient eastern monarch's search for a sentence that was "true and appropriate in all times and all situations." What his wise men presented to him was, "And this too shall pass away."

"How much it expresses!" Lincoln said. "How chastening in the hour of pride. . . . And yet let us hope that it is not *quite* true." Let us hope rather that "we shall secure an individual, social, and political prosperity and happiness, whose course shall be onward and upward, and which while the earth endures shall not pass away."[38]

Today, such a statement of hope, staked out in the very jaws of mortality, would be rare, if not inconceivable. As I said earlier, John W. Gardner raised the question of an "ever-renewing society" and called for "a Department of Continuous Renewal," but his discussion has not been joined. "How can we design a system that will continuously reform (i.e., renew) itself," he asked, "beginning with presently specifiable ills and moving on to ills that we cannot now foresee."[39]

Yet current American confidence smacks of the cocksure and the complacent rather than realism, and it relies on the capacity of public relations to conjure up reality through branding and image makeovers. So Americans trust in endlessly recycled slogans such as "renewing the American dream," "restoring the American promise," "the best is yet to be" and "America's future will always be greater than her past"—as if saying so could make it so. And it is striking how the notion of sustainability has become common in such fields as economic growth and development, and in relations with the environment, yet few Americans think about sustainable freedom.

Perhaps this is not surprising. Americans have always shown a strain of resistance to the idea of the open-endedness of the American experiment and the vulnerability of American freedom. Yet the challenge of open-endedness at the heart of the American experiment cannot be shuffled off so easily, for it is far earlier and stronger even than the framers. It is ultimately rooted in a realistic reading of history and in both the biblical and the classical views of the world that shaped Western civilization, not to speak of a tragic view of life.

The clearly Christian notes in this challenge to choice and open-endedness can be heard out in the Atlantic on the decks of the *Arbella* even before the colonists landed at Massachusetts Bay. But those notes look back millennia to the story of the Jewish people. John Winthrop's famous sermon "A Model of Christian Charity" was built on the precedent of the great challenge of Moses to the Jews in Deuteronomy. One way forward, Moses declared, leads to life, to health and to blessing; the other way to death, to sickness and to a curse. The choice had consequences, but the choice was theirs. Destiny was not determinism.

So Winthrop also urges his fellow adventurers approaching New England that they could carry out "the cause between God and us," enter into "the covenant," take up "the commission" and experience success—or they could turn aside to their own ends and condemn themselves to be a "shipwreck." They could be "a city upon a hill" or "shall be made a story and a by-word through the world."[40]

There is choice, there is challenge, and there are consequences. There are always two ways things can go—advance or decline—and there are always two levels at which to watch their condition. As Montesquieu and Tocqueville both pointed out, freedom may be maintained at the level of the Constitution but still be lost at the level of the citizens.

Liberty is therefore a marathon and not a sprint, and the task of freedom requires vigilance and perseverance if freedom is to be sustained. If the revolution's winning of freedom was a matter of eight years and the Constitution's ordering of freedom was completed in thirteen years, the challenge of sustaining freedom is the task of centuries and countless generations, including our own.

OLD DEBATES STILL RUNNING

These three tasks of establishing a free society—winning freedom, ordering freedom and sustaining freedom—are fundamental to understanding and appreciating the historic achievement of the founders. But, as I said earlier, they are also beguiling because of the issues they obscure. Freedom sounds simple, straightforward and self-evident. What could be more wonderful than the ability to do what we want? But freedom is both more complex and more contested than many realize, so those who would guard freedom with care must regard freedom with respect. "A rose is a rose is a rose," as Gertrude Stein said famously, but there is more to freedom than simply saying freedom is freedom is freedom.

The framers' success with freedom was so stunning that it makes the tasks look simpler than they were. Americans should therefore step back and ask how America's quest for freedom fits into some of the centuries-old debates about the character of freedom, and then ask what this means for the challenge of sustaining freedom today. Two debates in particular are important.

The first is the long-running debate over the difference between internal and external notions of freedom. Here the framers' position appears to be obvious, though on further scrutiny it is less so. Internal, or spiritual, freedom is the freedom that can be achieved by individuals regardless of their external circumstances. There, in the inner world of the mind and heart, is a space that no grand inquisitor, no government goon and no Google tracker can investigate or invade. There, no one can keep us from thinking, loving, believing, hoping or hating entirely as we wish.

Diverse religions and philosophies, such as Buddhism, Stoicism and the Christian faith, despite their fundamentally different views of the world, all agree on an insistence that genuine freedom requires internal freedom, not just external freedom. Such inner freedom is better than inalienable; it is illimitable and inviolable. To be free there is to be truly free.

Take the Stoic philosophers. Epictetus, for example, claimed that though he was a slave, he was freer than his master because he was able to rise above his chains. In his essay "On the Shortness of Life," his fellow Stoic Seneca argued that the exiled sage was better off in his humble shack than the preoccupied rich in their high-roofed dining halls. The early Christian apostle Paul made a similar argument for slaves on behalf of Christian freedom. Compared with such a profound and lasting freedom, the unfreedom of their fetters was irrelevant. Earlier still, Gautama Buddha called for a detachment and right-mindfulness that touched on the same freedom from outward circumstances. In very different ways, each of these faiths equated salvation with this inner freedom.

In contrast, it is often said that the American founders had absolutely no interest in internal, or spiritual, freedom. What they wanted was external, political freedom, which meant the freedom to speak and to act in the community and in particular to speak and to act in the public square without undue restraint.

Unquestionably the founders' goal was political liberty, and for those who prize political liberty, there are two problems with internal freedom alone. On the one hand, it is only half a freedom. On the other, when considered solely by itself, it can be misused and turned into a justification for being content with internal freedom alone and so can become the enemy of external freedom. It can be a rationale for political resignation and worse.

The criticism of internal freedom is simple. If we cannot get what we want and we are taught to want only what we can get, either we may become more realistic and mature or we may be sold a seductive rationale for resignation, masochism and slavery. Jean-Jacques Rousseau was at least right about this: better to face up to one's chains than to deck them with flowers and pretend they are not chains.

Yet this criticism is not the whole story. It does not do justice to the framers' full position, and it would be foolish to dismiss internal freedom too quickly. Needless to say, external liberty was the full goal of the American Revolution. But the dignity of the individual has a primacy over society and the state; the internal liberty of the individual is the primary and indispensable freedom; and in the form of freedom of conscience it was actually the first liberty for the framers (as we will explore in the fourth chapter). This in itself should be enough for us to take it more seriously, but its importance needs to be appreciated today for another reason.

We are rapidly reaching the point in Western consumer societies where people confuse freedom with choice, as they are dazzled daily by an ever-expanding array of external choices in consumer goods and lifestyle options. But the pursuit of freedom has led to a surfeit of choices and a scarcity of meaning and value—a point at which choice itself, rather than the content of any choice, has become the heart of freedom. The result is that modern people value choice rather than good choice.

Meanwhile, the imperatives of the consumer economy and the blandishments of marketing drive people ever faster. First they appeal to their sense of needs, then they touch their desires, and finally they play on their very wishes. Thus true freedom recedes as more and more "free choices" become more and more trivial, and the drive to consume grows ever more frantic and the production of waste ever more damaging.

As this spiral becomes vicious, the importance of sales resistance through inner, spiritual freedom rises again and becomes to the American republic a way to escape the golden handcuffs. Think of the corrupting effect of Rome's "bread and circuses," which power-hungry rogues such as Julius Caesar began to use even in republican days. If giving people what they want is the sure road to people wanting to be told what they want, then knowing what they need and what they ought to want is a first step toward freedom.

The story is told of Socrates walking through the market in Athens, with its groaning abundance of options, and saying to himself, "Who would have thought that there could be so many things that I can do without?"[41] His remark would apply even more to the contemporary American shopping malls. In early American history, internal freedom was expressed beautifully in the Shaker song "'Tis the Gift to Be Simple, 'Tis the Gift to Be Free," and more wryly in our time by Kris Kristofferson and Janis Joplin as "Freedom's just another word for nothin' left to lose."

Spiritual freedom is in fact a vital part of political freedom and its requirement for self-control, self-restraint and self-government. America may soon reach the point where political freedom—not to mention a trash-laden planet—can be saved only by a spiritual freedom strong enough to say no to false consumer freedoms that lead only to debt and the endless accumulation of junk and waste.

A TALE OF TWO FREEDOMS

A second long-running debate concerns the difference between negative and positive freedom. This argument can be traced back to debates in the Middle Ages, but it was made famous in the modern world by philosopher Isaiah Berlin's 1958 lecture "Two Concepts of Liberty."[42] Negative freedom, as Berlin defines it, is freedom *from*—in essence, freedom from interference and constraint. Positive freedom is freedom *for*—in essence, freedom for excellence according to whatever vision and ideals define that excellence. The framers' position here is also clear and balanced, but contemporary Americans have abandoned it. They have voted unambiguously for negative freedom rather than positive and have therefore exalted freedom as an essentially private matter, for where else can a person be truly free *from* all outside interference?

Berlin spoke in Oxford as a Jewish émigré who had seen the horrors of Stalin's Communism, and his two main examples of positive freedom were taken from European history: Roman Catholicism and communism. With such a background, he viewed positive freedom negatively, and he opted unashamedly for a preference for negative freedom.

Berlin's categories are useful, but the discussion that flows out of them is often unsatisfactory because in reality the choice between the two freedoms is never either/or. Negative and positive freedoms can be distinguished in theory, but if true freedom is to flourish, they must never be divorced in practice. Indeed, one of the most difficult challenges of the modern world is to create societies that allow diverse faiths and ideologies to have the maximum of both positive and negative freedoms for each faith and ideology. No nation has so far achieved full success in this test, though some have done better than others.

For one thing, neither positive nor negative freedom is complete without the other. They each describe complementary sides of the same full freedom, which always rests on two conditions: the complete absence of any abuse of power, which is the essence of negative freedom, and a vision of a positive way of life, which is the essence of positive freedom. In a free society understood in this way, free citizens are neither prevented from doing what they should (the denial of positive freedom) nor forced to do what they shouldn't (the denial of negative freedom).

The American road to freedom illustrates the importance of both dimensions. Negative freedom—in America's case, freedom from colonial rule—was foundational and indispensable, but by itself inadequate. Freedom *from* had to progress to freedom *for*, or else there would have been no point to freedom. As we saw, winning freedom was only the first step on the road to full freedom, so that living free depended on both ordering and sustaining freedom, both of which contained powerful visions of positive freedom.

Put simply, the goal of the American Revolution was not just independence but full freedom—both independence from the British and freedom to be Americans and to build the American republic. Stress negative freedom alone, however, and freedom becomes focused on private life, where negative freedom will always be strongest. But the term *private*, as Augustine pointed out sixteen centuries ago, is linked at its root to *privation* and *deprivation*. So the recent exaltation of freedom as a private matter has inevitably meant the degradation of freedom as a public matter, and the loser has been the American republic and its requirements for citizenship.

This point should not be reduced to a conservative/liberal argument. Importantly, the counterbalancing emphasis on positive freedom was once a liberal theme too. In the words of Henry David Thoreau in his *Journal*, "Do we call this the land of the free? What is it to be free from King George the Fourth and continue slaves to prejudice? What is it to be born free and equal and not to live? What is the value of any political freedom, but as a means to moral freedom?"[43] After all, as he wrote later in *Walden*, "It is hard to have a southern overseer, it is worse to have a northern one; but worst of all if you are the slave driver of yourself."[44]

In short, negative and essentially private freedom is never enough by itself, and certainly not for citizens of a republic. Positive freedom is essential too. Yet today both American conservatives and liberals often speak as if negative freedom were all—the only difference between them lying in what each considers the bogeyman from which there needs to be freedom. Liberals view freedom as freedom from the imposition of others ("Not with my body, you don't") and conservatives as freedom from government encroachment ("Don't tread on me" and "Get the government off our back").

The founders were wiser. It is certainly true that freedom can flourish only where there is no abuse of power and that the expansion-seeking will to power requires firm checks and balances rather than just virtue. "It is an eternal experience," Montesquieu wrote, "that every man who has power is drawn to abuse it; he proceeds until he finds the limits."[45] But that said, freedom is still always more than simply being freed and having abuse of power checked. True liberty is a state of life beyond liberation. In Tocqueville's words, it is not enough when "the body is left free, and the soul is enslaved."[46]

At the same time, freedom *for* will always ring hollow and remain incomplete for those who do not know freedom *from*, so the revolution's winning of freedom came first, and it had to. The Constitution could only strengthen what the revolution had secured. Freedom required independence. Liberty had to be preceded by liberation.

EACH DISTORTED IN ITS OWN WAY

Not just one but both of the two freedoms can be distorted, and each distortion can be dangerous in its own way. There are as many pitfalls in negative freedom as in positive freedom. Berlin was right that many of the great evils of history have been done in the name of one positive freedom or another, each coercing all others into the mold of its idealistic vision. The worst recent examples of such coercion are Soviet and Chinese Communism and Taliban Islamism.

Americans must realize, however, that in the eyes of many people around the world, America's interventions in the name of universal democratic freedom are also an assertive form of positive freedom—especially when "democratic freedom" is used to justify displays of American military power as if the cause of freedom were universally self-evident. After all, no positive freedom is self-evident except to those who believe it. Even "humanitarian intervention" is not self-evident. It happens to be the term Hitler used to justify invading the Sudetenland and Mussolini used to justify his seizure of Ethiopia. Humanitarian intervention that is just must first be morally justified. It is never self-evident.

At the same time, Americans must also remember that unconstrained negative freedom can be just as destructive as positive freedom and needs to be guarded against from two directions. To begin with, unconstrained negative freedom can easily degenerate into apathy and moral callousness, for what begins as freedom from interference easily slides into *the freedom of indifference*—"I am happy to be left to myself, so why should I care about others?" Thus emancipation from the constraints of others quickly becomes an evasion of concern for others. "I don't care what you do" becomes "What happens to you is no business of mine," so that no one is their brother's keeper.

Equally, freedom from interference starts as the concern to do what we each want to do, which becomes unconcern about what others want to do, which becomes unconcern even when others do what is harmful and wrong to themselves or others. To paraphrase Burke, the only thing necessary for the triumph of evil is for good people to do nothing because they do not wish to judge or intervene because they have only a negative view of freedom. Whereas Sierra Leone was founded by William Wilberforce and his friends as a safe haven for freed slaves, several American states had less worthy beginnings. Florida was admitted to the Union in 1845 as a slave state and showed its intentions clearly in the proposed motto for its flag: "Let us alone." Texas, which still thrives on its sturdy self-reliance and its "Don't mess with Texas" attitudes, was founded partly as a safe haven for the liberty of slaveholders.

As Abraham Lincoln pointed out, the Civil War was a clash between two freedoms: the negative freedom of the South and the positive freedom of the North. Today's liberal and libertarian supporters of negative freedom should ponder a simple but stunning fact: from the banning of infanticide in the Roman Empire, to the abolition of slavery in the British Empire, to the advance and protection of civil rights in America, none of the great liberal reforms of the West could have succeeded on the basis of negative freedom alone, and none will be launched on such a basis in the future. Liberals, without a respect for positive freedom, your liberalism is not as liberal as it needs to be.

In addition, negative freedom can become a license for unconstrained power. It is highly dangerous because what provides no limits to power provides no security for freedom. As such, negative freedom for the powerful leads easily to dominance and then to oppression of others (the freedom of imposition), whether in the unconstrained freedom of a spoiled child, a playground bully, a domineering boss, an unopposed political party—or an unregulated free market and an overdominant superpower.

Is there still any doubt that most of the founders did not advocate maintaining freedom through virtue alone? Sometimes the problem is that virtue alone is too weak. But at other times the worse problem is that unchecked virtue is too strong. As Montesquieu warned, "The soul takes so much delight in dominating other souls; even those who love the good love themselves so strongly that there is no one who is not so unfortunate as to still have reasons to doubt his own good intentions."[47]

In short, beware excessive and unchecked virtue, whether conservative or liberal. For clearly, the vice of unchecked virtue infects liberals too. Few things are more comic and hypocritical than the liberal who goes into convulsions over proselytizing religious believers who "impose" their beliefs on others, but who himself advocates some "right" or "truth" so fundamental that it is plainly a failure in enlightenment not to declare it "universal" and impose it on everyone everywhere, regardless of the wishes of the recipients. The plain fact is that few people in power are so truly good as to be able to doubt the pure benevolence of their own virtues or to scrutinize the self-evident benefits with which they would like to enlighten everyone else.

Checks and balances are of course the whole point of competition in a market and of a constitutional separation of powers in a republic—as the framers developed the notion from Montesquieu and the English Settlement of 1688, and as Madison argued so cogently in Federalist Paper No. 51. Unless rival competes with rival, power counteracts power, and ambition checks ambition, one person's unrestrained freedom will be a weaker person's unrestrained oppression. Then the peaceable kingdom will be impossible. The lamb can never lie down with the lion, for freedom for the lion will mean death for the lamb. Or in Benjamin Franklin's pithy version, "Democracy is two wolves and a lamb voting on what to have for lunch. Liberty is a well-armed lamb contesting the vote."

The same note can be heard in the anguished protest of the tiny Melians in the path of imperial Athens, in the defiance of the Jewish resistance to the Romans at Masada, in the resentment and indignation of the nineteenth-century Chinese in the face of European gun-boats, in the heart-rending cry of the American Indians before the expansive westward thrust of what Jefferson called the Empire of Liberty, in the world outrage in response to the United States insisting that both the interests of its freedom and of its actions-in-the-name-of-freedom gave it a right to unilateral action in Iraq. The lesson of all these incidents is the same: dominance on its own terms always appears self-evident to the dominant, but what is unrestrained freedom and power for one is humiliation and oppression for others.

UNDER THE JUDGMENT OF HER OWN IDEALS

As I said and will say again, America stands before the world today under the judgment of her own ideals. Again and again it is Montesquieu and Madison, rather than Marx and Muhammad, whose principles boomerang back on America in world reactions to America's superpower actions. As I have heard argued by foreign admirers of the U.S. Constitution at universities in Europe, Asia and the Middle East, it is hypocritical for Americans to pride themselves on checks and balances at home but to ride roughshod over international opinion, institutions, laws and other checks and balances abroad, or to talk of free-market capitalism and impose it on others in a coerced, lopsided manner favorable only to American corporations and investors.

Over the centuries, Britain stood with coalition after coalition against the threats of "universal monarchy" represented variously by Louis XIV, Napoleon and Hitler, all in the interests of the balance of power. In the same way, it is of little surprise that many in the world wish to counter U.S. dominance today. Benign, star-spangled dominance is still dominance and needs checks and balances no less.

Ironically, American liberals and radicals who attack American aggression abroad often espouse the same negative view of freedom at home that they deplore abroad. In fact, what unites an otherwise disparate group that would include most liberals, almost all libertarians and most postmodern radicals is that freedom is largely a question of escaping the power of others over them. It is all about dismantling the structures of oppression and liberating the victim.

But what then? What freedom is to mean for the liberated is not a concern and no one else's business. But then we are back to the core conundrum of freedom. Freedom requires a framework of order, which means restraint, yet the only restraint proper to freedom is self-restraint, which freedom undermines.

Whatever positions we take on such issues, these old debates about freedom are a valuable corrective to naivety and utopianism. The passion for freedom is simple and strong, but freedom itself is subtle, complex and demanding. Its defense is never simple and easy, never a matter of arms alone. While the world still turns and the boot of the powerful still grinds into the faces of the weak and poor, the human cry for freedom will never be silenced and the bell of freedom will always ring out along with the cries of suffering and anger.

Equally, cries for justice and for order will always blend with cries for freedom, and it will always be harder to be free than not to be free. Freedom's work is never alone and never done, which is why the founders' confidence in the prospect of a freedom that could remain free forever is so audacious and so deserving of greater attention than it is given by a free people grown complacent through the privileges of freedom.

"Who dares wins," runs the famous motto of Britain's Special Air Service. The American revolutionaries dared and the American revolutionaries won, and it is up to the heirs of that freedom to rise to the challenge of that dare and to shoulder the burden of that duty across the vast tracks of time. For again, Americans should never forget: all who aspire to be Rome in their beginnings must avoid being Rome at their ending. Rome and its republic fell, and so too will the American republic—unless . . .

3

USING HISTORY TO DEFY HISTORY

ROMAN GENERALS DID NOT CRY. But Publius Cornelius Scipio Aemilianus Africanus Numantinus, hero of the final Punic War, victor over Carthage and scion of the noble house of the great Scipio Africanus, was weeping openly as Carthage burned in front of him.

For the better part of half a century, Rome had breathed a sigh of relief after her victory over Hannibal and his elephants in the Second Punic War, and then debated endlessly as the final showdown with Carthage loomed closer. From one side, Cato the Elder, the scourge of Carthage, had ended every speech to the Senate with his signature closing, "And I, for my part, think that Carthage must be destroyed!" ("*Carthago delenda est!*") From the other side, equally on cue and without fail, Scipio Nasica had risen to reply, "And I, for my part, think that Carthage should be left standing."

Most senators of that time sided with Cato, fearful that Carthage's reviving commerce would enable her to be a military rival to Rome again. So the Romans, vengeful and untrusting, eventually found their pretext and declared war on the hapless Carthaginians, who this time stood no chance—especially when command of the Roman forces was given to the brilliant, ruthless, young Consul Scipio Aemilianus, grandson by adoption of Hannibal's conqueror. In the spring of 146 B.C., after six days of brutal street fighting, the walls were breached, and Rome's forces were free to wreak their will on the defenseless citizens, many of whom were slaughtered and the rest sold into slavery.

Overriding Scipio's objection, the Roman Senate ordered that the city be plundered, razed and burned—and the story was later added that the ruins were sown with salt. It was at some moment during the ten days that Carthage burned, with one magnificent building after another collapsing into rubble and ashes, and the pall of smoke hanging over the ruined city like an angel of death, that Scipio Africanus the Younger wept over Carthage.

Was Scipio overwrought? Was he frustrated with orders with which he had long disagreed? He had warned that if Rome destroyed Carthage and was left unchecked, she would ride roughshod over smaller states and would finally disintegrate internally through her own unchecked factionalism and self-interest—as eventually happened under the Caesars. His friend and tutor Polybius, who was standing by his side, knew what he was thinking. As Polybius recorded later in his *Histories*, Scipio "stood long reflecting on the inevitable change which awaits cities, nations, and dynasties, one and all, as it does every one of us men."[1]

For when Scipio had given the orders to torch the city, "he immediately turned around and grasped me by the hand and said, 'O Polybius, it is a grand thing, but, I know not how, I feel a terror and dread lest someone should one day give the same order about my own native city."[2]

How extraordinary, Polybius reflected, that such a great man on the day of his greatest success should have been aware of the "mutability of Fortune" and its eventual reverse. Troy had fallen. The once mighty empires of the Egyptians, Assyrians, Babylonians, Persians, Greeks and Macedonians had each vanished in its turn. Carthage was burning in front of him, and however long delayed,

Rome's time would come, as indeed it did. Scipio had achieved a victory for the ages, but he needed no slave to whisper in his ear, "This too shall pass."

NO HOLIDAY FROM HISTORY

My old headmaster used to say to me that the entire history of Rome can be captured in three stories about the Scipio family. The above story is the middle one, and the other two underscore the same point about the transience of life and the passing of empires and superpowers.

The earlier story took place in 190 B.C. when the elder Scipio, Africanus, led the Roman armies into Asia on their first imperial foray. He was met by Heraclides of Byzantium, the ambassador of the Seleucid emperor, who urged the Romans to think twice before they embarked on a fateful extension of their rule that would one day lead to their undoing.

"Let the Romans limit their empire to Europe," Heraclides said, and then added words that apply to all empires and superpowers, including the United States, "that even this was very large; that *it was easier to gain it part by part than to hold the whole.*"[3] The Romans brushed him aside on that day, but true to his warning, Rome expanded and expanded and expanded "part by part" until she was overextended and fell, as all the world's empires and superpowers have done in their turn. Each was once strong, confident, proud and here to stay, and each in its turn has gone.

The last story is Cicero's "Dream of Scipio," which is recounted in his *On the Republic.* He pictures an imaginary meeting between the two Scipios—grandfather and grandson—before the final Punic War, with the younger Scipio dreaming when he fell asleep. His vision was of the smallness and short-lived transience of the world seen from the perspective of outer space—long before the Apollo landing brought photos from the moon that showed how tiny and fragile our little, hanging, blue ball of an earth is. Scipio said,

> As I looked around from my vantage point in every direction, the whole earth was complete and beautiful. I saw stars never seen from the earth, larger than anyone has ever imagined. . . . The earth in fact seemed so minute in relation to these spheres that I began to think less of this vast Roman Empire of ours which is only a pinpoint on the surface of this small earth.[4]

A pinpoint on earth and a blink in time—the American founders were well acquainted with these classical views of flux, change, transience, decline and decay. In fact they deliberately built the country to counter such pessimism—and they did so with a realism born of an equally intimate understanding of history.

Here we come to the highly distinctive feature of the genius of the founders—one that sets them apart from most contemporary Americans. Seeking to create a free society that would remain free, they learned from history. In fact, *they used history to defy history*. Thus, like the ancients, they took history seriously. But unlike the ancients, who saw time as cyclical, they were shaped by the linear worldview of the Bible and the Enlightenment. Thus, like contemporary Americans, they were optimistic. But unlike most Americans today, their optimism was never at the expense of a holiday from history.

As founders, they addressed their hour, but they were never merely creatures of their moment. Knowing that the power of the past lies in its continuing presence, they engaged their times with success because they knew so well all that had been thought and done before. In this sense, the founders were as rooted as they were revolutionary. As Madison wrote proudly in Federalist Paper No. 14, "Is it not the glory of the people of America that whilst they have paid a decent regard to the opinions of former times and other nations," they have not "suffered a blind veneration for antiquity?"[5] Far from slavishly copying the past, they learned from the past in order to dare to build a republic for which there was no precedent in the annals of history. In their attitude toward history, they were following "a new and more noble course."[6] They were truly a *novus ordo seclorum*, a new order of the ages.

This emphasis on the founders' sense of roots is largely lost today, passed over in favor of the revolutionary character of their work. But it deserves far greater recognition. Above all, it provides a grand corrective to two common American myths: that Americans are entirely a practical, self-made people rather than theoretical and reflective in the European manner, and that the framers' ideas sprang out of nothing but their own original thinking. The golden fact is that the founders were fully modern but had a profound classical sense of the wisdom of the ages.

The Stoic philosopher Seneca wrote of the maturity of the sage who knows how to annex every age to broaden the perspective of his own. And Bernard of Chartres wrote in the twelfth century of the debt we owe to our ancestors: "If we see more and further than they, it is not because of our own clear eyes or tall bodies, but because we are raised on high by their gigantic stature."[7]

The exiled Niccolo Machiavelli actually changed into his best clothes to enter into his nightly reading conversation with the ancients. Later, Tocqueville claimed that Pascal, Montesquieu and Rousseau were "three men with whom I live a little bit each day."[8]

Just so the founders entered into a rich dialogue with the writers from the classical world and became the wiser for it. After all, as T. S. Eliot observed in defense of such wisdom, "Someone said: 'The dead writers are remote from us because we know so much more than they did.' Precisely, and they are that which we know."[9]

Jefferson, for example, for all his dislike of England, held that Francis Bacon, Isaac Newton and John Locke were "the three greatest men that have ever lived, without any exception," and he hung their portraits as his heroes in his study at Monticello.[10] Equally, the works of Plato, Aristotle, Thucydides, Polybius, Cicero, Virgil, Horace and

Seneca were as common in the speeches of the founding generation as they were in their libraries.

Today's best-selling biographies of the revolutionary generation are enough to show that most Americans do not join Henry Ford in pronouncing history as "bunk." But from the abysmal depths of public education to popular attitudes toward newer-is-truer and latest-is-greatest, the United States demonstrates the distinctively modern obsession with the present and the future at the expense of the past. Progress, choice, change, novelty and now the new buzzword *innovation* are the hot/cool/in/trendy/must-see/must-have desirables in a consumerist society. The past, almost by definition, is passé, out-moded, dusty and "so yesterday." After all, as the mindless business saying goes, "There are only two kinds of businesses (or politics, churches or nations): those that are changing and those that are going out of business."

"We Americans seem to know everything about the last twenty-four hours," journalist Bill Moyers remarked, "but very little of the past sixty centuries or the last sixty years."[11]

Change for change's sake is of course pointless and destructive—in a word, nihilism. The wisdom of the ages quietly points elsewhere. Times may change, and with them kingdoms and empires, but human nature stays the same, so the past is the enduring guide to the present. Consider these thoughts regarding the past:

Montesquieu wrote, "To comprehend modern times well, it is nec-essary to comprehend ancient times well."[12]

Goethe remarked similarly, "He who cannot draw on three thousand years is living hand to mouth."[13]

"A people with no memory of its past is like a mature man who has lost all recollection of his youth," Tocqueville wrote down from a lecture by Francois Guizot.[14]

"The longer you can look back, the further you can see forward," Winston Churchill observed.[15]

"Decay of libraries is like Alzheimer's in the nation brain," the poet Ted Hughes wrote.[16]

Clearly the framers sided with the wisdom of history. Patrick Henry, far from the leading intellectual among the founders, acknowledged, "I have but one lamp by which my feet are guided, and that is the lamp of experience. I know of no way of judging the future but by the past."[17]

But the real proof does not lie in amassing quotations. It can be seen in the careful way the founders used history to fashion a political system to defy the pessimism that seemed to be the melancholy lesson of history. Nowhere is this plainer than in the founders' understanding of freedom. If Americans were to become free, live free and remain free forever, they would have to do so in light of a sharp understanding of the classical menaces to freedom.

ALL WE CAN DO IS BE VIGILANT

To the classical authors, the first menace to freedom is the obvious one: an external menace (which today's scholars inelegantly call "exogenous shock"). Suddenly, whatever its system of government and however peaceful its intentions and policies toward its neighbors, a nation can find itself threatened from the outside by another nation's hostility or by a range of hostile forces, as the Romans were by the barbarians. All that such a nation or empire can do under these circumstances is to remain vigilant and armed, forging the necessary alliances that will complement its strategic strengths and offset its strategic weaknesses.

Writing of governments facing this threat of hostility from the outside, Polybius remarked laconically, "The external admits of no certain or fixed definition," and passes on.[18] In other words, there is not much that some nations can do. The menace may come in any number of forms and alliances. Inevitably, small nations will always be more vulnerable than large and powerful nations, but not even Rome was immune, as the Goths and Visigoths demonstrated in A.D. 410.

That is surely the reason why the threat of external hostility was never the prime concern of the founders. The majority of them were Englishmen who came from a small, protected island and who then lived on a large, protected continent. They were blessed with a natural buffer of the earth's two largest oceans and were confronted by a generally weak and defenseless native population. They were granted the historic opportunity to expand to a continent-sized nation and were endowed with extraordinary human and natural resources. So as the founders of the young American republic—warned by Washington to be ever cautious about "entangling alliances"—they were safer than any nation in Europe from which Americans came or were to come.

That was then. In a day of intercontinental ballistic missiles, jet planes, the World Wide Web and globalized crime and terrorism, that benign estimate has changed forever, dramatically symbolized by September 11 attacks on the World Trade Center and the Pentagon. The two-ocean buffer, so much stronger than a European border post or the twenty-one-mile English Channel, is still vital to America's homeland security, but external menace is now a prime concern.

It was not so for the framers. In Washington's "Farewell Address" in 1796, he said briefly, "Observe good faith and justice toward all Nations. Cultivate peace and harmony with all," and then spent most of his speech on internal menaces.[19]

In the same tenor, when Lincoln addressed "The Perpetuation of Our Institutions" fifty years later, he was almost cavalier about an external threat. "At what point shall we expect the approach of danger? By what means shall we fortify against it?" he asked. And then, within living memory of the imperial menace of Napoleon, he continued:

Shall we expect some transatlantic military giant, to step the Ocean, and crush us at a blow? Never!—All the armies of Europe,

Asia, and Africa combined, with all the treasure of the earth (our own excepted) in their military chest; with a Buonaparte [*sic*] for a commander, could not by force, take a drink from the Ohio, or make a track on the Blue Ridge, in a trial of a thousand years.[20]

The exhilarating taste of that optimism returned briefly in the years after 1989 and the end of the Cold War. With no serious challenges to American dominance and no serious threats to American security, the sky looked cloudless. "I'm running out of demons, I'm running out of enemies," Colin Powell said when he was chairman of the Joint Chiefs of Staff. "I'm down to Castro and Kim Il Sung."[21] Little did he realize what would come out of the skies on September 11. However, just a year after those attacks, Stephen Walt of Harvard would still claim that "the United States is the most secure great power in history."[22]

It should be neither a surprise nor a concern that the founders did not foresee today's world and did not take this external menace seriously. Knowing what the founders knew of history as well as what we know of history since them, the greater concern is that today's generation overlook the next menace, which they took more seriously than any external threat.

THE CORRUPTION OF CUSTOMS

To the classical authors, the second menace to freedom is less obvious but more lethal, because it is self-generated and almost unavoidable: a corruption of customs. Here we have to pause deliberately to make sure the point is understood before it is dismissed. For many modern minds, the idea that "culture matters" is a foreign one, and like anything foreign, it is commonly dismissed as alien. After all, the presumption runs, culture is only for conservatives and social scientists. What really matters is what is rational, economic, legal, scientific and technological.

The classical understanding of the corruption of customs deserves to be understood, and it was used in various ways. Plutarch used it to explain the fall of Sparta, just as Sallust did to account for the decline of the Roman republic and as people on different sides did to explain the fall of the Western Roman Empire in A.D. 410—the pagans (and later Edward Gibbon) blaming the Christians, and Augustine and the Christians blaming the pagans.

At the core of the classical understanding was an acute sense of historical irony and an assumption that is the exact opposite of most people's today: Nations are most vulnerable, not when they are weak, but when they are strong. For unless guarded vigilantly, prosperity leads to hubris (the presumption of invulnerability), hubris to folly and folly to nemesis, or self-induced judgment. The moment of success is the moment to be most vigilant. Careless celebration is rife with mortal peril.

The classic expression of this view was on the Greek stage, and it was applied to great individuals, such as the tragic heroes of Aeschylus, Euripides and Sophocles. They were blinded by their success and plunged from invincibility to the suffering that was the tragic reminder of their human limitations. In terms of nations, the fullest account of the classical understanding, and the one with which the framers grappled, was that of Polybius in his *Histories*. He was, after all, the same Polybius who was tutor to Scipio Aemilianus, witness of the sack of Carthage, historian to Rome and an inspiration to the American framers. Both Madison and Jefferson cite the book as a very important ancient influence on the founding of the American republic.

Polybius surveyed all the forms of government that he could find. Like Aristotle, he classified them according to six basic types, categories that Cicero followed in his own later discussion. The first three represent the healthy form of government: monarchy, the rule of one, a king or queen; aristocracy, the rule of the few, or the excellent; and democracy, the rule of the many, or the people. The other three represent the corrupt form of the same government: tyranny, the degenerate form of monarchy; oligarchy, the degenerate form of aristocracy; and mob rule, the degenerate form of democracy.

Using this analysis, Polybius sets out three key claims. First, what is decisive for any nation is the form of its constitution, the fundamental laws that embody its character and culture. "Now in every practical undertaking by a state we must regard as the most powerful agent for success or failure the form of its constitution."[23] Each nation's constitution is the fountainhead of all its successes and failures and the deepest expression of the very character of its life.

Many Americans are so accustomed to self-congratulatory references to the U.S. Constitution that they stop at this first thought and go no further. But Polybius goes on: second, whatever system of governance a nation adopts and whatever its constitution, it will always be subject to a process of change. In fact, there is "ordained decay and change" or "a natural cycle of constitutional revolutions" as nations rise, prosper and fall. Anyone who understands this cycle of "growth, zenith, and decadence" is able to follow what is "the regular cycle of constitutional revolutions."[24]

Third, this cycle of change is so clear and observable that if anyone takes the trouble to understand it and its causes, they would be able to apply the insight to the history of any nation and assess accurately where the nation is in its cycle of growth or decline at any moment. "He perhaps may make a mistake as to the dates at which this or that will happen to a particular constitution," Polybius said, "but he will rarely be entirely mistaken as to the stage of growth or decay at which it has arrived, or as to the point at which it will undergo some revolutionary change."[25]

Here is where the classical understanding of the second menace comes in, and the point that Americans often forget today. The reason for this constant cycle of revolutions, Polybius said, lies in the fact that a nation's constitution, though decisive for its form of government, is not sufficient by itself to sustain it forever. A constitution rests on a foundation. Or more accurately, it rests on a bedding of customs, traditions and moral standards, from which it grows and by which it is sustained. So the character and health of these customs is crucial, for some customs are positive, healthy and therefore supportive of the constitution, and others are negative, degenerate and hostile. "Desirable" customs make the private lives of citizens virtuous and the public character of the state "civilized and just," whereas "objectionable" customs are damaging.[26]

Any corruption of customs is therefore deadly serious for a nation, and no constitution by itself can ensure the permanence of a nation if its customs degenerate. Polybius's famous paragraphs describing how customs are corrupted is sobering for its description of the state of power and prosperity in great nations just prior to their decline. They stand as a commentary on the great empires of the past and a caution for the United States today.

> When a commonwealth, after warding off many great dangers, has arrived at a high pitch of prosperity and undisputed power, it is evident that, by the lengthened continuance of great wealth within it, the manner of life of its citizens will become more extravagant, and that the rivalry for office, and in other spheres of activity, will become fiercer than it ought to be. And as this state of things goes on more and more, the desire of office and the shame of losing reputation, as well as the ostentation and extravagance of living, will prove the beginning of a deterioration.
>
> And of this change the people will be credited with being the authors, when they become convinced that they are being cheated by some from avarice, and are puffed up with flattery by others from love of office. For when that comes about, in their passionate resentment and acting under the dictates of anger, they will refuse to obey any longer, or to be content with having equal powers with their leaders, but will demand to have all or far the greatest themselves.

And when that comes to pass the constitution will receive a new name, which sounds better than any other in the world, liberty or democracy; but in fact, it will become that worst of all governments, mob-rule.[27]

Cicero was always equally emphatic about the internal danger. Probably his most quoted lines are from the opening words of his attack on the Cataline conspiracy: "O tempora! O mores!" ("Oh the times! Oh the ways of life!") In that speech to the Senate at the trial of Rabirius, he declared bluntly, "No external or foreign threat can infiltrate our Republic. If you wish Rome to live forever and our empire to be without end, if you wish that our glory never fade, we must be on our guard against our own passions, against men of violence, against the enemy within."[28]

Years later, in the early eighteenth century, Montesquieu differed openly from the classical and Renaissance vision of republicanism and its reliance on virtue. But when it came to the menace of corruption, he was in full agreement: "It is a thing singular: the more these states have of security, the more, like waters excessively tranquil, they are subject to corruption."[29] Worse still, when success breeds prosperity and prosperity luxury, and luxury prevails, "it marks the end for a republic."[30] Thus—in a classic statement of how "more is less" when it comes to freedom—"the more they draw advantage from their liberty, the more they approach the moment when they will lose it."[31]

Once again, John Gardner underscored the same point, but his voice is rarely listened to by modern Americans. "No system of social arrangements, no matter how cleverly devised, no matter how democratic in character, is adequate to preserve freedom unless it is undergirded by certain habits and attitudes which are shared by members of the society."[32]

This classical realism spells out immense lessons for the United States today. Internal problems are more dangerous than external, success is more corrupting than failure, peacetime can be more dangerous than war, habits of the heart are as important as laws, and the greatest menace is not the external enemy but what Cicero called "the enemy within." For however virtuous and clear-sighted any of us may think we are, which of us is strong enough to argue against our own successes and strengths? So, what an external enemy can do in a moment, the corruption of customs can equally do over time—which leads to the third menace.

THE INJURIES OF TIME

To classical authors, the third menace was the most unrelenting and least avoidable of all: *passing time.* The founders who read Montesquieu knew that it was a great challenge to create a large republic, a republic on a continental scale. But the greatest challenge of all was to create a *lasting* republic, one that would defy not only the decades, but also the centuries. Curiously, however, this is the menace about which many modern Americans are least interested. It now takes a determined effort for modern Americans to see things as the founders saw them and feel about them as they felt, not only in terms of their individual lives but also for the life of their nation and their political arrangements.

Reflect for a moment on the situation today. In the global era and in the Internet galaxy, the twin currencies of today's way of life are connectivity in terms of information and mobility in terms of people. The global world has an essentially democratic capacity for communication that has shifted from the few to the many to the many to the many, and it has a near-godlike capacity to be instant, immediate, everywhere and all at once. People today also have the capacity to conduct their affairs anywhere in the world regardless of time, place and government.

We are therefore the first generation to live in a round-the-clock, live-coverage world, to be able to follow world events as they happen, and to be able to encounter everywhere in the world from anywhere else and at any time. But the result of this near-miracle of the instant and the immediate is that many have fallen for an illusion. They have mistaken the compression of space and time for the conquest of space and time.

It is true that, to an unprecedented degree, modern people have conquered space with jets, cell phones, texting, Skyping, tweeting and worldwide, satellite-based communications. In this sense we can legitimately talk about the end of geography and about annihilating time in some areas and distorting it in many others. Distances no longer matter as they did once; boundaries and walls no longer keep people in or keep people out; and age-old categories such as short and long, close and far away, have changed forever.

But no one has conquered time, and Hegelian talk of the end of history is fatuous. Mechanical clock time, first industrialized and then computerized in the modern 24/7 world, has all but conquered humans, and it grows more powerful still as communication accelerates to the speed of light. Not in spite of but because of our technologies of speed and our labor-saving devices, we have less time and more pressure than ever before, even at the ordinary level of living.

More seriously still, among the speed-effects of modern fast-life, modern people are driven toward a necessary automation that undermines the possibility of human deliberation and decision, thus hollowing out serious journalism, responsible politics and the very possibility of statesmanship. The near-irrelevance of the U.S. Congress in the face of the Iraq War and the Wall Street crisis was telling.

The result is drastic. As Paul Virilio, the eminent analyst of speed, comments: "The more speed increases, the faster freedom decreases."[33] Yet oddly people rarely ponder the speed and shortness of it all or the fact that focused attention is their rarest commodity, time is their most expensive luxury, and both are becoming ever more precious.

The ancients were under no such illusions. Even in a slower-moving world, they knew well that time flows. Life moves on. The years pass by. The running centuries run on tirelessly. One by one the sands of time slip through the hourglass inexorably. Advance is always possible, but loss is absolutely certain. Consider these thoughts on the passing of time:

"All flesh is grass," cried the Hebrew prophet Isaiah.

We cannot step in the same river twice, the Greek philosopher Heraclitus observed.

Everything in life is "turmoiled by our master Time," Sophocles lamented.

"The spider is the curtain holder in the palace of the Caesars," Sultan Mehmet observed with sorrow as the conqueror of Constantinople.

"Certainly it must sometime come to pass that the very gentle Beatrice will die," wrote the Italian poet Dante.[34]

"Time, like an ever-flowing stream / Bears all its sons away," wrote Isaac Watts, the hymn writer so loved by the early colonists.

For all of us, the time is short and the span of life is brief. On top of that, our real human problem, the Stoic philosopher Seneca said in a direct rebuke to the modern illusion, is not just that life is short but that we waste so much of it—so that life ceases for us "just when we are getting ready for it."[35]

But whether wasted or used well, Seneca said, life is still short and measured always against the merciless march of time. In Thomas Hardy's poignant self-description, we are each a "time-torn man," caught between the wrenching pull of the rhythms of nature on one side and the regulated world of manmade social time on the other.[36]

And what is true of individual human lives is also true of our greatest human accomplishments, including nations, forms of government and the monuments and memorials designed to preserve their memory. In the end, remorseless time devours them all. Seneca concluded, "Honors, monuments, whatever the ambitious have ordered by decrees or raised in public buildings are soon destroyed: there is nothing the passage of time does not demolish and remove."[37]

When Cicero was fighting Rome's fateful shift from the early republic to the empire of the Caesars, he lamented the ravages of time on the great city of Romulus and Remus. What was once fresh had faded. What had been revolutionary had become routine. The republican rhetoric was still there, but its once-robust reality had gone. The form was unaltered, but the substance had vanished without a trace.

> But our age, having received the commonwealth as a finished picture of another century, but already beginning to fade through the lapse of years, has not only neglected to renew the colors of the original painting, but has not even cared to preserve its general form and prominent lineaments.
>
> For what now remains of those antique manners, of which the poet said that our republic consisted? They have now become so obsolete and forgotten, that they are not only not cultivated, but they are not even known. . . . For it is owing to our vices, rather to any accident, that we have retained the name of republic when we have long since lost the reality.[38]

The ancients' view of time was stern, but it needs to be heard by Americans today. "History devours its own children," it was said. "Whatever it brings forth passes away someday." Each form of government, whatever its defining principle, will finally be carried to excess. It will then breed a reaction to itself and end up, like Shelley's Ozymandias and the Sphinx near Cairo, as a ruin in the sand and a caution to generations that come after it. Lord Acton commented that even Tacitus confessed that the mixed form of constitution, so loved by men of ideas (and later by the American founders), "however admirable in theory, was difficult to establish and impossible to maintain."[39]

For all their Enlightenment optimism, the greatest thinkers of the eighteenth century were no strangers to the idea of passing time. "If Sparta and Rome perished," Rousseau wrote, "what state can hope to endure for ever?" The year 1787 witnessed not only "the miracle in Philadelphia," but the publication of the last volume of Edward Gibbon's classic *The History of the Decline and Fall of the Roman Empire*. "This spectacle of the world," the great historian mused in the last chapter describing the Palatine Hill in Rome, "how it is fallen! How changed! How defaced! The path of victory is obliterated by vines, and the benches of the senators are concealed by a dunghill."[40]

Indeed, as Gibbon contemplated the grass growing, the cattle grazing and the dunghill concealing where once our mighty Romans deliberated, his first answer to why Rome fell was simple: "the injuries of time and nature." Or as he went on more expansively in a strongly classical tenor, "The art of man is able to construct monuments far more permanent than the narrow span of his own existence: yet these monuments, like himself, are perishable and frail; and in the boundless annals of time his life and his labors must equally be measured as a fleeting moment."[41]

The same somber note can be heard in Lincoln's Lyceum address. Fifty years after the revolution, he cautioned that the "living history" of the revolution—and the tempering of destructive passions—was beginning to fade because of "the lapse of time." The veterans who were the living memories of the revolution are gone. "They *were* a fortress of strength; but, what invading foemen could *never* do, the silent artillery of time *has* done; the leveling of its walls."[42]

Again, in Lincoln's address in Wisconsin on September 30, 1859, he told of the Eastern monarch who asked from his wise men a sentence that would be "true and appropriate in all times and situations" only to receive the words "And this, too, shall pass away." To which Lincoln mused in response, "And yet let us hope it is not *quite* true. Let us hope, rather, that by the best cultivation of the physical world, beneath us and around us; and the intellectual and moral world within us, we shall secure an individual, social, and political prosperity and happiness, whose course shall be onward and upward, and which, while the earth endures, shall not pass away."[43]

Yet again, in July 1880, when the great Egyptian obelisk was lowered at great cost and with great effort onto its 220-ton pedestal near the newly built Metropolitan Museum of Art in New York, Secretary of State William Evarts sounded out the warning it conveyed to the Gilded Era: "Can you expect to flourish forever? Can you expect wealth to accumulate and man not to decay?"[44] (Two years earlier, President Grant's wife, Julia, had remarked on seeing the Sphinx, "One could not but reflect here on the emptiness, frailty and vanity of the works of man."[45])

AS ALIEN AS A MARTIAN

Such realism is not completely absent in America more recently. Walter Lippmann reminded Americans that "when Shakespeare was alive there were no Americans, that when Virgil was alive there were no Englishmen, and that when Homer was alive there were no Romans."[46] At best, as historians point out, the United States is in its very early days as a superpower. As I write these words, the United States is a little over 230 years old, which is exactly half the age of Rome when Julius Caesar crossed the Rubicon, the event that, though it drove the stake into the heart of the old republic, ushered in the long centuries of Rome's imperial greatness.[47]

Such thoughts would be alien or gloomy to most Americans today. They would never fit into campaign sound bites or be a serious theme in a State of the Union address—which today has descended into a theatrical event with applause-cued lines jerking congressmen, senators and cabinet members to their feet like puppets on a string. The idea of learning from Gibbon's "injuries of time," Lincoln's "silent artillery of time" and his "all-resistless hurricane" of time sits oddly with both modern and postmodern American ways of thinking. But such was ever the way with hubris and the presumption of invulnerability.

Modern people believe that labor-saving technologies and instantaneous communication have brought them closer to conquering time as they have conquered space. According to such thinking, they are increasingly masters of their lives, their world and now even of time itself. Do they not have perpetual health and sustainable life almost within their grasp, both for themselves and for their institutions?

Against such foolish thinking, the plain fact is that progress in science and technology does not mean progress in morality and humanity. But, not surprisingly, utopian blueprints and blithe progressivism have both flourished along with the wonders of modern scientific progress. George W. Bush's remarks on universal freedom and the end of tyranny sit well with such empty dreams. For rather than inching forward by patient, incremental advances, the illusion of unstoppable progress drives forward on the notion of the absolutely clean slate and the total self-confidence of the Grand Masters of the Present. Is it not the privilege of Americans or democrats or capitalists to design the Future with a capital F once the past has been wiped clean?

"History is more or less bunk," Henry Ford said, or if his infamous remark is given its fuller statement, "We don't want tradition. We want to live in the present and the only history that is worth a tinker's damn is the history we make today."[48] Or in the words of Holroyd, a wealthy American in Joseph Conrad's *Nostromo*, "Time itself has got to wait on the greatest country in the whole of God's universe. . . . We shall run the world's business whether the world likes it or not. The world can't help it—and neither can we, I guess."[49]

Such absurd and pompous balderdash aside, will history make an exception and allow America to fulfill its utopian dreams? Will time stand still for the United States any more than it did for Britain, France, the Netherlands, Spain, Rome or Greece? Will the stones of the Washington Monument escape the fate of the Parthenon, the pyramids and the Hanging Gardens of Babylon? Will the giant figure of Lincoln in his memorial last longer than the Roman Consuls on whose curule chair he was placed?

The very questions stagger the mind for anyone with a sense of history, but to the modern mind, history as the remembered past is of little account and need not be considered seriously. The notion of even a practical past is passé. After all, as the poet Wendell Berry writes derisively, "The Future is where we'll all be fulfilled, happy, healthy, and perhaps will live and consume forever."[50]

THE TYRANNY OF NOW

The postmodern mind, in contrast to the modern, is obsessed with relativism and fragmentation. In this view, time is neither linear nor cyclical. It is pointillist—like truth and certainties of all kinds, it is pulverized into a thousand scattered points, each unrelated to the others and to the past and future. There is no building on the past to construct the future. There is no building at all. In fact, there is no duration, bond, tie or commitment. There is only the endless succession of the fleeting now and its array of endless choices that open the future. So there are only separate moments, episodes rather than stories, fragments rather than building blocks, shifting kaleidoscopes rather than meaningful narratives. "No ties, no tears," is the press release of the modern nomads ever restless to "move on" through the sad deserts of their consequence-free wandering.

In such a world, dominated as ever by consumerism and driven by the nihilistic but still fashionable philosophy of change for change's sake, the old is obsolete and the past is a ball and chain. The new is by definition always the "new and improved," and the art of forgetting is more important than remembering and learning. Protean flexibility has replaced the wisdom born of precedent and experience. The timeless is what lasts ten years. Know-how has been overshadowed by know-who and know-who-to-be. And loyalties born of commitment have become a liability rather than an asset.

Even relationships are renewable in short-term increments now. They are not like traditional marriage's "until death do us part" but are limited extensions like those of a magazine subscription or a phone card. For, as far as possible, each moment must be all-new, a fresh possibility, a new choice, a blank DVD ready to record the future with the past wiped clean. The delete button is always only a click away. Today in America, when "till death do us part" has shrunk to "as long as love lasts," even marriages are severed with a text message.

The outcome of the confusion between America's modern and postmodern views of time is a tangle of contradictions. We are witnessing the emergence of a generation that both forgets the past and favors and fears the future. We are seeing people becoming accustomed to an attitude that says, "Time is money," but so hate to waste time that they change faster and faster, until the breathless pace of change makes enjoying anything impossible.

Americans today are building a society with a passion for all that is ephemeral, disposable and throwaway, yet they still absurdly presume that prosperity and freedom will remain permanent. When time seemed hardly to move and the world looked durable, the word to the wise was what they were apt to forget: *momento mori*. But now, when everything changes quickly, nothing lasts longer than a few seconds, and we are constantly urged to *carpe diem* if life is not to slip from our grasp, people still presume that their freedom will somehow last forever—without a thought as to how.

In America's "instant society," what is instantaneous is also immediate and therefore intense, and the result is the tyranny of now.

Obsessive, round-the-clock, live coverage of disasters and horrors such as September 11, the Columbine school shootings, Hurricane Katrina and the great Gulf oil spill may leave them reeling, but it is easy to comprehend and addictive to watch. It is the must-see fare of today's twenty-four-hour cable networks and their invitation to gawk at life and its disasters and sorrows. But the real dangers are opaque, for time erodes freedom in slow motion. Liberty is never lost all at once.

Without a doubt, the founders are closer to the optimism of the modern mind than to the pessimism of the postmodern, though for them the optimism had to be found on the other side of realism—a confidence wrested from the very jaws of history, which gave them both a reliance on the past and a confidence in the future.

Whether modern optimism can be sustained without the realism of first facing history remains to be seen. But those who profess such modern confidence, as well as those who feel the pains of postmodern pessimism, owe it to themselves to understand the founders' optimism as well as their solution of using history to defy history. After all, if the ancients and the founders were correct, the only alternative to their approach is decline.

All of today's preachers of American freedom, from the presidents down, should ponder what their founders built knowingly into the foundations. The ultimate test of freedom is not the economy or the military, but time. Freedom's ultimate trial is mortality, and the essence of mortality is flawed human nature. History is not just for scholars, but also for citizens as humans. The study of history as "how the present came to be" or a saying such as "The past is prologue," which is carved on the wall of the National Archives in Washington, D.C., is often misunderstood as a grandiose version of "It's all about us"—as if the present generation is the grand crescendo of everything that has gone before as they bask in the bliss of their Eternal Now.

Lenin's famous questions "Who? Whom?" apply not only to power but to time. So Americans must never fall for the delusions of presentism. They must always ask whether they are living as if their ancestors were the dawn to their noon or whether their present lives turn the present into a feeble afterglow of a greatness that has gone. There are times in history when the past is the prelude to a glorious present, but there are many more times when the present is merely the postscript to a far more glorious past.

What "the past is prologue" really means is that our generation, while standing on the shoulders of those who have gone before and being all the wiser for their wisdom, is plunged into the relentless currents of time that rush us forward together. The present generation is vulnerable to its force; we too shall pass, and no account of "the state of the union" that ignores these truths can amount to more than an idle daydream. Forget this history-born realism, and Americans will one day fade from history still muttering by rote that their best and brightest days are still to come—as if saying it made it so.

It is always a pleasurable challenge to speak like this of history, for unlike the world of today that leaves history to the historians, the founders' age knew the folly of engaging the present without the light of the past. It is time for such wisdom again. For Americans must never forget: all who aspire to be like Rome in their beginnings must avoid being like Rome at their ending. Rome and its republic fell, and so too will the American republic—unless . . .

4

The Golden
Triangle of Freedom

I am always intrigued by how few Americans
know the account of what has been called the most important unknown moment in American history and the single most important
gathering ever held in the United States: the incident in which America's most noble Cincinnatus refused the title of "George I of the
United States" offered him by the Continental Army in Newburgh,
New York, toward the close of the Revolutionary War.

After the decisive victory over Lord Cornwallis at Yorktown in
1781, the army had moved into quarters near Newburgh to wait for
the peace settlement. But without the war to concentrate on, various
states had failed to meet their obligations to the army, and the Continental Congress had grown remiss in paying the soldiers to whom it
owed its success. In many cases payments were years in arrears, pen-
sions were in question altogether, and the soldiers feared that Congress would simply disband the army and default on its promises. Not
surprisingly, the camp had become a breeding ground for bitterness
in which talk of treason and sedition was rife.

In short, in 1782 the American Revolution had reached the stage characteristic of many republics and revolutions at which a dangerous vacuum of power had built up. The obvious way forward was for a strong man to step in and stop the slide toward chaos by wresting the situation to his will—as Julius Caesar did in Rome, Cromwell in England, Robespierre in France and Lenin in Russia.

All those men did, but not George Washington. Letters and signed and unsigned papers began to circulate through the camp, stirring the restless dissatisfaction, as did whispering that the only solution to the "weakness of republicks" was a military dictatorship and that there was only one man fit for such rule. But the first commander in chief would have none of it. When one of his own officers, Lewis Nicola, wrote to him saying that they would be better off with him as king, he flatly turned the thought aside: "Be assured, Sir, no occurrence in course of the War, has given me more painful sensations than your information of there being such ideas existing in the army as you have expressed."[1]

Yet the angry talk swirled around Washington unabated, and the festering mutiny came to a head on March 15, 1783, when the general surprised the conspirators by entering their officers' assembly and urging them strongly to turn back from such folly. Using three different lines of argument, he hit a brick wall each time and ended looking out on faces as stony and unresponsive as when he began. But then, just when it looked as if he had failed, he tried to read a letter from a Virginia congressman and fumbled for a pair of spectacles no one had ever seen him wear before—"Gentlemen," their fifty-one-year-old leader said wearily after eight years in the field, "you will permit me to put on my spectacles, for I have not only grown gray but almost blind in the service of my country."[2]

Whether spontaneous or contrived, Washington's simple symbolic act accomplished in a second what all his arguments had failed to do, and there was hardly a dry eye as the general walked out of the tent, mounted his horse and rode away. As Major Samuel Shaw reported at the time, "There was something so natural, so unaffected, in this appeal as rendered it superior to the most studied oratory." The incident was a non-event that was more decisive than most events. The American Revolution would not go the way of other revolutions. Washington was as victorious over the temptation to Caesarism at Newburgh as he had been over the British at Yorktown.[3]

FIRST, FIRST, FIRST

George Washington truly was "the indispensable man" of the American Revolution, as historian James Flexner described him, and he was so by force of his character rather than his ideas or his eloquence. In this and other similar incidents, he was a one-man check and balance on the abuse of power, and decisively so well before the Constitution framed the principle in law.

Earlier Montesquieu had underscored the rarity and importance of such moderation in leaders: "Great men who are moderate are rare: & it is always easier to follow one's impulse than to arrest it . . . it is a thousand times easier to do good than to do it well."[4] Jefferson wrote in the same vein, "The moderation and virtue of a single character probably prevented this Revolution from being closed, as most others have been, by a subversion of that Liberty it was meant to establish."[5] Similarly, Abraham Lincoln wrote later, "Nearly all men can stand adversity, but if you want to test a man, give him power."[6]

Even Washington's adversary George III was impressed. When his royal portrait painter, Jonathan Trumbull, told the king that Washington intended to retire to his farm after the Revolutionary War was over, he was surprised. "If he does that," the king remarked—and Washington went on to do it not once but twice—"he will be the greatest man in the world."[7]

Such heroic character shone brighter still when Washington became the first president. Then when he retired and died soon after, the tributes soared higher and higher until he was first elevated into the Moses who had led his people out of bondage and then—in "the apotheosis of Washington"—divinized as the creator, savior and father of his people. In the more straightforward words of Congressman Henry Lee at his memorial service, he was "first in war, first in peace, first in the hearts of his countrymen."[8] Far more, John Adams added, "For his fellow citizens, if their prayers could have been answered, he would have been immortal."[9]

Excessive adulation of this sort, and the impulses toward a powerful civil religion that lay behind it, are rightly suspect today. But those who are zealous in debunking them often go to the other extreme and miss their real significance. For the founders, Washington's exemplary character was not just the happy fluke of an exceptional individual at an opportune moment or even the social product of a young nation's subconscious search for a center of national unity to replace an overthrown king. Its significance was at once simpler and more profound: character, virtue and trust were a vital part of the founders' notion of ordered liberty and sustainable freedom.

THE GORILLA IN THE ROOM

Two things have consistently surprised me in my years in the United States: that the sole American answer to how freedom can be sustained is the Constitution and its separation of powers and that the rest of the founders' solution is now almost completely ignored.

It was not always so. Historians point out that the modern elevation of the Constitution as the sole foundation and bulwark of American freedom reached its present height in the 1930s. That was no accident. Significantly, it came right on the heels of a general secularization of American law that has led in turn to a general legislation of American life. The preceding decades were the time when legal contracts were strengthened and sharpened to take the place of weakening moral considerations such as character and trust (the "my word is my bond" of an earlier time).

Significantly the elevation of the Constitution also came after long periods of surprising earlier neglect. Michael Kammen has even written of the recent "cult of the Constitution" and of "the discovery of the Bill of Rights." The motto of the American Liberty League in 1936 stated this elevated view beyond doubt: "The Constitution, Fortress of Liberty."

I have no quarrel with that tribute, but its timing and its context are revealing. The U.S. Constitution and all legal contracts were elevated at the very moment when faith, character, virtue and trust began to be denigrated and relegated to the private sphere. The framers' famous separation of powers between the executive, the legislature and the judiciary is unquestionably distinctive and fundamental to the American vision of enduring freedom. But as an answer to how freedom must be sustained, it is neither an original solution nor the founders' complete solution.

For one thing, even the separation of powers was once far stronger than it is today. It originally included a robust view of the rights and powers of local government to balance the power of the states and of the rights and powers of the states to balance the rights and powers of the federal government. Tocqueville saw the first of these as the seedbed of American freedom and Alexander Hamilton praised the second as "a double security to the people."[10] Needless to say, this entire dimension has been seriously emasculated, starting with responses to the Civil War and accelerating through the deliberate centralization of government under the Progressives and the Depression-era leaders—and climaxing in the last decade.

All in all, this radical loss of local American self-government and the unchecked growth of centralized federal government has been the result of three things: the old evils such as slavery and the new dangers such as terrorism that made it necessary; the new technologies and procedures such as computerized bureaucracy that made it possible; and the new ideologies such as progressivism that made it desirable. The Fourteenth Amendment and its consequences, for example, were the steep but understandable price of rectifying the Constitution's greatest flaw: the blind eye turned toward slavery. To be sure, the federalizing trend was therefore necessary and inevitable, but the lack of a careful, compensating devolution to restore the balance of individual self-reliance and local self-government is inexcusable. And the result is inescapable: the full system of checks and balances that the founders designed has gone.

For another thing, as I have repeated so often because it is even more often ignored, the great European commentators stressed that freedom in modern societies must be maintained and assessed at two levels, not just one: at the level of the Constitution and the structures of liberty, and at the level of the citizens and the spirit of liberty. Focusing solely on the separation of powers at the level of the Constitution is sobering enough, but it misses an equally important slippage at the level of citizens.

The framers also held that, though the Constitution's barriers against the abuse of power are indispensable, they were only "parchment barriers" and therefore could never be more than part of the answer. And in some ways they were the secondary part at that. The U.S. Constitution was never meant to be the sole bulwark of freedom, let alone a self-perpetuating machine that would go by itself. The American founders were not, in Joseph de Maistre's words, "poor men who imagine that nations can be constituted with ink."[11] Without strong ethics to support them, the best laws and the strongest institutions would only be ropes of sand.

Jefferson even argued with Madison, who strongly disagreed with him, that because the earth belongs to the living, "no society can make a perpetual constitution. . . . Every constitution then, and every law, naturally expires at the end of 19 years. If it be enforced longer, it is an act of force, and not of right."[12]

More importantly, as Judge Learned Hand declared to new American citizens in Central Park, New York, in 1944: "The Spirit of

Liberty" is not to be found in courts, laws and constitutions alone. "Liberty lives in the hearts of men and women; when it dies there, no constitution, no law, no court can even do much to save it. While it lives there, it needs no constitution, no law, no court to save it."[13] The nation's structures of liberty must always be balanced by the spirit of liberty, and the laws of the land by the habits of the heart.

All of which means there is a deep irony in play today. Many educated people who scorn religious fundamentalism are hard at work creating a constitutional fundamentalism, though with lawyers and judges instead of rabbis, priests and pastors. *Constitutional* and *unconstitutional* have replaced *orthodox* and *heretical*. But unlike the better angels of religious fundamentalism, constitutional fundamentalism has no recourse to a divine spirit to rescue it from power games, casuistry, legalism, litigiousness—and, eventually, calcification and death.

So reliance on the Constitution alone and on structures and laws alone is folly. But worse, the forgotten part of the framers' answer is so central, clear and powerful that to ignore it is either willful or negligent. What the framers believed should complement and reinforce the Constitution and its separation of powers is the distinctive moral ecology that is at the heart of ordered liberty. Tocqueville called it "the habits of the heart," and I call it "the golden triangle of freedom"—the cultivation and transmission of the conviction that freedom requires virtue, which requires faith, which requires freedom, which in turn requires virtue, which requires faith, which requires freedom and so on, like the recycling triangle, ad infinitum.

In short, sustainable freedom depends on the character of the rulers and the ruled alike, and on the vital trust between them—both of which are far more than a matter of law. The Constitution, which is the foundational law of the land, should be supported and sustained by the faith, character and virtue of the entire citizenry, which comprises its moral constitution, or habits of the heart. Together with the Constitution, these habits of the heart are the real, complete and essential bulwark of American liberty. A republic grounded only in a consensus forged of calculation and competing self-interests can never last.

NO STRAW MEN, PLEASE

Before we go a sentence farther, let me be absolutely plain. It would be a cardinal error not to recognize the originality of the modern liberal republicanism of the majority of the American founders and its crucial difference from two other positions: the classical republicanism of Greece and Rome and the republicanism of the so-called devils party led by Machiavelli, Francis Bacon, Thomas Hobbes and others.

The founders' position was a significant advance on the earlier conception of the relationship between freedom and virtue. In the opening sentence of his *Discourses on Livy*, Machiavelli professed himself to be a revolutionary innovator like Christopher Columbus and Amerigo Vespucci, who discovered "new modes and orders."[14] But it was the founders' generation that gave the world the real "new order of the ages" (*novus ordo seclorum*), and their vision was in direct and deliberate contrast not only to the classical republicans of Greece and Rome, but also to Machiavelli and his disciples.

Ironically, the great Florentine used to harp on about the purported realism of his insistence on "the effectual truth of the matter," in contrast with the utopianism of the republics of Plato and others.[15] But in the name of realism, he was highly unrealistic, as are many contemporary American advocates of realpolitik who ignore the place of human fallibility and the limited but proper place of virtue.

Put differently, between the old orders of Athens, Sparta and Rome, and the new order of the ages wrought in Philadelphia lay not only two millennia in time but a chasm in thinking led by such revolutionaries as Machiavelli, Montaigne, Bacon and Hobbes. Among many differences, one is striking above all. Whereas liberty for the Greeks and the Romans was supremely a matter of political reason, virtue and what they did in public life, for modern people it is also and even more a matter of what is done in private life, and there is less place for public reason and the common good, and none at all for virtue.

To be sure, Jefferson argued strongly for classical republicanism. He believed, along with many classical, Renaissance and some Enlightenment republicans, that the newborn American republic could and should be sustained by virtue alone, especially the virtue that was bred by farming and stewardship of the land. (Montesquieu wrote, "The Greek political writers, who lived under popular government, acknowledged no other force able to sustain them except that of virtue."[16])

In strong contrast, the authors of *The Federalist*, along with other liberal republicans, were insistent that in a commercial republic, as opposed to a classical republic, virtue alone could never sustain freedom and that commerce was as important as farming for cultivating virtue. There could be no simple-minded mimicking of the Greeks and Romans, Hamilton declared. "We may preach till we are tired of the theme, the necessity of disinterestedness in republics, without making a single proselyte . . . it is as ridiculous to seek for models in the simple ages of Greece and Rome, as it would be to go in quest of them among the Hottentots and Laplanders."[17]

Americans today have gone to the opposite extreme from Jefferson's, and one that the founders disapproved of equally. If reliance on virtue alone is an unrealistic way to sustain freedom, so also is reliance on a constitutional separation of powers alone. If liberty is to endure, the twin bulwarks of the Constitution and the golden triangle of freedom must both play their part. To replace "virtue alone" with "no virtue at all" is madness, and what the Wall Street crisis showed about unfettered capitalism could soon be America's crisis played out on an even more gigantic screen. Leadership without character, business without ethics and science without human values—in short, freedom without virtue—will bring the republic to its knees.

To put the point more broadly, in human affairs there will always be a limit to the plannable, the legislatable and the regulatable, and only the fool or a utopian will try to leap over this built-in boundary. Or as T. S. Eliot wrote famously in his play *The Rock*, it is folly to dream of "systems so perfect that no one will need to be good."[18] Down that way, and at the point where our brave new realists are foolishly unrealistic, lies disaster for America.

NOTHING LESS THAN
THE REAL THING

More still must be said about the proper place of virtue in guarding freedom. First, *some* virtue (rather than virtue *alone*), along with checks and balances, will always be needed because humans play what Aristotle called a "double game"—or in the biblical perspective are "fallen" and represent Kant's "crooked timber of humanity." We humans act politically, inspired not only by faith, virtue, courage, honor, excellence, justice, prudence, generosity and compassion, but also by self-interest, self-preservation, power, greed, vanity, revenge and convenience—and wise governance must take both sides into account.

In Rome, there was a divided consulship to keep power from falling into the hands of a single dictator, though the clearer American separation of powers is required to offset the foolish idealism of trusting in virtue alone. But substantive virtue—and not only a separation of powers—is required to offset the dangerous realities of the negative side of the human double game. Checks and balances by themselves will never be enough.

Second, this urgent and very practical need for substantive virtue calls into question two strategies that some Americans count on to fill in for the loss of virtue. Both have worked in the past, but neither will work today if there is no place given to virtue at all.

One false strategy is to rely on the faux virtue that in a democracy can parallel the faux honor that Montesquieu described in a monarchy. ("In well-regulated monarchies, everyone will be something like a good citizen while one will rarely find someone who is a good man."[19]) Where there is at least lip service paid to virtue, as Rochefoucauld observed famously, "hypocrisy is an homage that vice pays to virtue," so that hypocrisy may sustain a semblance of virtue even where there is no real virtue. People "proud of hiding their pride" can parade their faux virtue of humility, and so on. Bernard Mandeville made the same point in *The Fable of the Bees*: "The nearer we search into human Nature, the more we shall be convinced that the Moral Virtues are the Political Offspring which Flattery begot upon Pride."[20]

Unquestionably, that possibility has worked well in the past. Machiavelli's originality was simply to turn the age-old practice of hypocrites into the new-fangled philosophy of statesmen and so to make "the appearance of virtue" operational rather than virtue itself. This, of course, is a pretend virtue that has no link to genuine virtue at all. Needless to say, this strategy has always been played on skillfully by hypocrites, demagogues and cynics alike.

But the pretense of virtue requires an essential condition: faux virtue, or hypocrisy, works when real virtue is honored, and there is enough of it to imitate in flattery. For that very reason, it will not work as well today because of a double handicap. On the one hand, much of the United States has reached the point where virtue is hardly esteemed at all, or at least not welcomed in the public square, and where vice is often flaunted—"greed is good," and the like. Where this is the case, there is no need for hypocrisy to flatter anything but itself, and the phrase "faux virtue" is redundant. On the other hand, under postmodern conditions, where knowledge is really power and everything is other than it appears, there is no point even to appear virtuous, for any true and straightforward virtue is impossible and not worth imitating.

The second possible form of substitute virtue is the sturdier pragmatic virtue that is driven solely by the requirements of commerce, a functional virtue parallel to the real virtues that Max Weber described as "the Protestant ethic." Such a virtue, or more properly *virtues*, was once real and powerful in America, and it provided the thrust that propelled America toward the heights of its economic prosperity. But it too has lost its strength in the contemporary world.

The empire of consumerism has undermined the Protestant ethic, and virtues such as delayed gratification have been shouldered aside by the clamor for instant gratification. And a prominent and almost comic feature of the American business world is the recurring spasms of concern about corporate ethics, though when the spasms have passed, what seems to have resulted is ever-tightening legal and regulatory compliance rather than character.

HACKLES RAISED

But who today acknowledges the gorilla in the room? Read the speeches and writings of the American founders on freedom, virtue and faith, and it is impossible not to notice a body of teaching that is clear, strong and central—themes that, as historian Bernard Bailyn observes, are "discussed endlessly, almost obsessively, in their political writings."[21] Yet somehow these themes are ignored today in the terms in which they were written. For, needless to say, the framers' position raises hackles in many circles, as will the present argument unless considered without prejudice.

For a start, the golden triangle links freedom directly to virtue. In a society as diverse as today's, that raises the question "Whose virtue?" and in an age that prizes toleration, it raises the specter of virtuecrats itching to impose their values on others. Worse still, the golden triangle links freedom indirectly to faith. I would soften that to a "faith of some sort," and broaden it to include naturalistic faiths, but it still prompts a barrage of instant dismissals that blows dust in the eyes of anyone trying to take freedom and the founders seriously.

One common line of dismissal is to say that the founders were not politically serious; they were only indulging in civic rhetoric for occasions such as July 4. Another is to say that they referred to religion and republicanism so often because they were children of their times, and their times were much more religious than today's. Yet another is to argue that, while the founders counted on faith to help sustain freedom, two hundred years later Americans have other points of reliance, so that freedom today no longer requires virtue, or virtue faith. Yet another line of dismissal is to say that, based on the contradiction between freedom and slavery, the founders were quite simply hypocrites.

MEN RATHER THAN ANGELS

All such objections are important and must be answered, but they are moot if Americans today do not understand the framers' golden triangle and its importance to sustainable liberty. Unquestionably the framers knew from history and their own experience that the wrong relationship of faith and virtue to freedom had been and would always be disastrous for both freedom and faith.

In addition, political philosophers earlier and elsewhere—most vociferously in France—had linked republicanism strongly with irreligion, along the lines we see today in France, Turkey and secularist totalitarian countries. An oppressive monarchy and a corrupt state church were seen as one and the same, and republicans longed to be rid of both. "Men will never be free," wrote the *philosophe* Denis Diderot, "until the last king is strangled with the guts of the last priest"—a cry that the Jacobins picked up and made into an imperative, translating the assertion from words into bloody deeds and laying the foundations of France's famed *laicite* today.

Beyond any question, the way the American founders consistently linked faith and freedom, republicanism and religion, was not only deliberate and thoughtful, it was also surprising and anything but routine. In this view, the self-government of a free republic had to rest on the self-government of free citizens, for only those who can govern themselves as individuals can govern themselves as a people. As for an athlete or a dancer, freedom for a citizen is the gift of self-control, training and discipline, not self-indulgence.

The laws of the land may provide external restraints on behavior, but the secret of freedom is what Englishman Lord Moulton called "obedience to the unenforceable,"[22] which is a matter of virtue, which in turn is a matter of faith. Faith and virtue are therefore indispensable to freedom—both to liberty itself and to the civic vitality and social harmony that go hand in hand with freedom.

Burke wrote in full agreement, "Manners [or moral standards] are of more importance than laws."[23] Rousseau had written similarly that mores, customs and traditions, which are "engraved neither in marble nor in bronze but in the hearts of the citizens" form "the true Constitution of the State" and the "Keystone" of a republic.[24]

Tocqueville emphatically agreed. His objective in writing *Democracy in America* was not to turn Frenchmen into Americans, for liberty should take many forms. "My purpose has rather been to demonstrate, using the American example, that their laws and, above all, their manners can permit a democratic people to remain free."[25]

People today who tout the superiority of their "realism," who espouse the Machiavellian view and who reject any place for virtue in favor of self-interest and self-preservation, should ponder the logic and lesson of the Civil War. As John Quincy Adams lamented, high ideals and cool judgment were on the side of freedom in the North, whereas passion and eloquence were on the side of oppression in the South. Why? The contrast demonstrated "how much more keen and powerful the impulse is of personal interest than is that of any general consideration of benevolence or humanity."[26] Neither the Civil War nor the civil rights movement could have been won on the basis of the philosophy of Machiavelli, Hobbes, Locke—or of today's postmodern thinkers.

But that said, the golden triangle of freedom must be stated with great care. For a start, the word *requires* in "freedom requires virtue, which requires faith" does not mean a legal or constitutional requirement. The First Amendment flatly and finally prohibits the federal government from requiring faith in any established way. But a proper and positive understanding of disestablishment leads directly to the heart of the framers' audacity: the American republic simultaneously rests on ultimate beliefs—for otherwise Americans have no right to the rights by which they thrive—yet rejects any official, orthodox formulation of what those beliefs should be. The republic will always remain an undecided experiment that stands or falls by the dynamism of its entirely voluntary, nonestablished faiths.

Also, the framers did not believe that the golden triangle was sufficient by itself to sustain freedom without the complementary safeguard of the constitutional separation of powers. That fallacy dogged many classical republics—they trusted too naively in virtue. As Madison warned, faith, character and virtue were necessary but not sufficient in themselves to restrain a majority from overriding the rights of a minority.

> What motives are to restrain them? A prudent regard to the maxim, that honesty is the best policy, is found by experience to be as little regarded by bodies of men as by individuals. Respect for character is always diminished in proportion to the number among whom the blame or praise is to be divided. Conscience, the only remaining tie, is known to be inadequate in individuals; in large numbers little is to be expected of it.[27]

Faith, character and virtue were necessary and decisive, but never sufficient by themselves. They must be balanced by the immovable bulwark of constitutional rights, especially for those in the minority.

Above all, the point must be guarded from a simple misunderstanding. The framers' near unanimity about the golden triangle of freedom did not mean that they were all people of faith or that they all agreed about the best way to relate religion and public life or that they were individually paragons of whatever faith and virtue they did espouse. In the language of Madison's Federalist Paper No. 51, they were "men rather than angels."

For a start, the framers demonstrated a wide spectrum of personal beliefs. Most were regular churchgoers, for whatever motive, but they ranged from orthodox Christians such as John Jay and George Mason to deists such as John Adams and Thomas Jefferson to freethinkers such as Benjamin Franklin.

In addition, the framers argued for different views of religion and public life, ranging from Patrick Henry's bill to support all churches to Jefferson's restatement of Roger Williams's "wall of separation." And as I stressed earlier, it is beyond question that several of them were distinguished for their vices and hypocrisies as well as for their virtues.

FREEDOM REQUIRES VIRTUE

Yet for all these differences, inconsistencies and hypocrisies, the framers consistently taught the importance of virtue for sustaining freedom, which is the first leg of the golden triangle: *freedom requires virtue.*

In December 2007, Governor Mitt Romney attempted to defuse the contentious place of his Mormon faith in his first presidential campaign. He asserted bluntly that "freedom requires religion."[28] Unsurprisingly, in the thick of the culture warring over religion and public life, this sentence set off a furious reaction. But such a bald statement is neither what the founders claimed nor how they expressed it. Freedom requires virtue, the founders mostly claimed, not religion.

Benjamin Franklin made a terse statement: "Only a virtuous people are capable of freedom."[29] Or as he stated it negatively in his famous maxims: "No longer virtuous, no longer free; is a maxim as true with regard to a private person as a Commonwealth."[30]

"Statesmen, my dear Sir, may plan and speculate for liberty . . . ," John Adams wrote to his cousin Zabdiel in 1776. "The only foundation of a free Constitution is pure Virtue, and if this cannot be inspired into our People, in a greater Measure than they have it now, they may exchange their Rulers, and the forms of Government, but they will not obtain a lasting Liberty."[31] Or as he wrote to Mercy Otis Warren the same year, "Public virtue cannot exist without private, and public Virtue is the only foundation of Republics." If the success of the revolution was to be called into question, it was "not for Want of Power or of Wisdom, but of Virtue."[32]

A key article in the influential Virginia Declaration of Rights in 1776 explicitly denies that "free government, or the blessings of liberty, can be preserved to any people, but by a firm adherence to justice, moderation, temperance, frugality, and virtue." New Hampshire went further, substituting for "virtue" "all the social virtues."[33]

As these quotations show, evidence for the first leg of the golden triangle is profuse—so much so that it is tempting to reach for one of the multitude of "quote books" that form part of the arsenals on either side of the culture wars. In contrast, works such as Edwin Gaustad's *Faith of the Founders* or James Hutson's *The Founders on Religion* establish the claim beyond argument but with the solid reliability of distinguished historians.[34]

CHARACTER COUNTS

Let me underscore the significance of the founders' arguments. They deserve deeper thought because they stand out so sharply from much opinion today. First, the reason for the need for virtue is simple and incontrovertible. Only virtue can supply the self-restraint that is the

indispensable requirement for liberty. Unrestrained freedom undermines freedom, but any other form of restraint on freedom eventually becomes a contradiction of freedom. For Burke, this was the
dangerous irresponsibility of the French freethinkers: "They explode
or render odious or contemptible that class of virtues which restrain
the appetites."[35]

Second, the founders went beyond broad general statements on
the importance of virtue to quite specific applications, such as the
need to integrate virtue in both private and public life. "The foundations of our National policy," George Washington wrote in 1783,
"will be laid in the pure and immutable principles of private morality" (a phrase repeated word for word in his first inaugural address in 1789).[36] "The foundation of national morality," John Adams
wrote similarly, "must be laid in private families."[37]

This tirelessly repeated conviction lay behind the framers' insistence on the importance of character in leadership. The golden triangle challenges the rulers as much as the ruled. In his "Dissertation
on the Canon and Feudal Law," John Adams directly addressed the
issue of preserving liberty. He concluded that the people "have a
right, an indisputable, unalienable, indefeasible, divine right to that
most dreaded and envied kind of knowledge—I mean of the char-
acters and conduct of their leaders."[38] Note the astonishing string of
words that today would be naturally associated with terms such as
freedom and *rights*, but which Adams applies to the citizens' right to
know the *character* of their leaders.

Were the framers correct that character counts in leadership? One
party in today's debate would dismiss their concern summarily. In a
day when followers are obsessed with rights and leaders with powers
and privileges, mention of virtues is irksome. And with religion
widely "privatized" and the public square increasingly considered
the realm of processes and procedures rather than principles, character and virtue are often dismissed as private issues. In the run-up
to President Clinton's impeachment, for example, educated opinion

was vociferous that the character of the president was irrelevant as a public issue. For all that many scholars cared, the president might have had the morals of an alley cat, but however shameless he was, his character was a purely private issue. What mattered in public was competence, not character.

But there is another party in the debate, one taught by history and experience to prize the place of character in leadership. Montesquieu even claimed that "bad examples can be worse than crimes," for "more states have perished because of a violation of their mores than because of a violation of the Laws."[39]

The story of the American presidency could teach this lesson by itself. "The destruction of a city comes from great men," Solon warned the Greeks. "It's not easy for one who flies too high to control himself."[40] "The passions of princes are restrained only by exhaustion," Frederick the Great remarked cynically about absolute monarchs. "Integrity has no need of rules," Albert Camus wrote more positively, and its converse is that no amount of laws and regulations can make up for lack of integrity in a leader.[41]

George Reedy, special assistant to Lyndon Johnson, looked back on his experience close to the Oval Office: "In the White House, character and personality are extremely important because there are no other limitations. . . . Restraint must come from within the presidential soul and prudence from within the presidential mind. The adversary forces which temper the actions of others do not come into play until it is too late to change course."[42]

One of the strongest but strangest endorsements of the importance of character comes from Richard Nixon. C.Q. (Character Quotient), he claimed, was just as important as I.Q. in political leadership and in choosing personnel.[43] Ironically, no one need look further than his own administration for graphic illustrations of his point. Led by Henry Kissinger and Alexander Haig, not to mention the president himself, the towering egos, prickly vanities, bitter jealousies, chronic insecurities and poisonous backbiting of his White

House virtuosi were a major factor in the tragedy of his undoing.

Character is far from a cliché or a matter of hollow civic piety. Nor is it a purely private matter, as many claimed in the scandal over Clinton's affair with a White House intern. History shows that character in leaders is crucially important. Externally, character is the bridge that provides the point of trust that links leaders with followers. Internally, character is the part-gyroscope, part-brake that provides the leader's deepest source of bearings and strongest source of restraint when the dizzy heights of leadership mean that there are no other limitations. Watching and emulating the character of leaders is a vital classroom in the schooling of citizens. "In the long run," James Q. Wilson concluded, "the public interest depends on private virtue."[44]

Whatever position one takes on the issue, it would be rash to dismiss the framers' position as empty rhetoric—not least because the framers expressly denied that it was. "This is not Cant," John Adams wrote to the same cousin, commending his teaching of virtue, "but the real sentiment of my heart."[45] That freedom required virtue, they believed, was a matter of political realism and a serious part of the new science of politics.

THE GREAT CONVERSATION

Third, the framers' conviction about freedom's need for virtue is part of their engagement with the great conversation that runs down the centuries from the Bible and the classical writers of Greece and Rome. To dismiss their point without realizing why and how they entered the conversation would be presumptuous, and to pretend today that we have no need for the wisdom of the great conversation would be foolish. For example, in May 1776, when John Witherspoon, president of Princeton and the "great teacher of the revolution," preached his landmark sermon on the eve of the revolution, he openly addressed the classical concern we saw in the previous chapter: the corruption of customs and the passing of time—both of which for him were the product of sin and the corruption of human nature.

In his support of the coming revolution, Witherspoon was bold and unequivocal: "I willingly embrace the opportunity of declaring my opinion without any hesitation, that the cause in which America is now in arms, is the cause of justice, of liberty, and of human nature."[46]

But as the only minister who was to sign the Declaration of Independence, Witherspoon was no jingoistic cleric indiscriminatingly sprinkling holy water on the muskets on the eve of battle. Instead he looked ahead to the moment after the euphoria of victory when citizens should appreciate the need for "national character and manners." Nothing is more certain, he warned, than that a corruption of manners would make a people ripe for destruction, and laws alone would not hold things together for long. "A good form of government may hold the rotten materials together for some time, but beyond a certain pitch, even the best constitution will be ineffectual, and slavery will ensue."[47] The golden triangle was not sufficient, but it was necessary.

George Washington's "Farewell Address" in 1796 engages the same conversation. Whether original to him or the work of Alexander Hamilton, his point is unmistakable: "Of all the dispositions and habits which lead to political prosperity, Religion and morality are indispensable supports. In vain would that man claim the tribute of Patriotism, who should labor to subvert these great pillars of human happiness, these firmest props of the duties of Men and citizens."[48]

Supports, pillars, props, foundations, wellsprings—Washington's choice of words tells the story by itself of how freedom requires virtue. But he too was aware of the classical understanding of decline and fall, and he addressed it directly even at that dawn-fresh moment in the new republic. "Can it be that Providence has not connected the permanent felicity of a nation with its virtue?" he asked rhetorically. To achieve such "permanent felicity," or Adams's "lasting liberty," he counseled them as "an old and affectionate friend" that they would need virtue to "control the usual current of the passions, or prevent our Nation from running the course which has hitherto marked the Destiny of Nations."[49]

If being a "nation of nations" means that Americans should have a wiser perspective on the wider world, then being the latest in the grand succession of superpowers means that Americans should also have a "history of histories" to offer a wiser perspective on the long reaches of time.

When Tocqueville came to write about America, he knew it would be difficult to rally his fellow Frenchmen to such an idea, but he would try nonetheless. As he wrote to Eugene Stoffels, a friend, "To persuade men that respect for the laws of God and man is the best means of remaining free . . . you say, cannot be done. I too am tempted to think so. But the thing is true all the same, and I will try to say so at all costs."[50]

By design or by neglect, Americans continue that great conversation today, and it would be the height of folly to pretend otherwise, which is precisely why it is easy for a visitor to enter these debates today, for they are not unique to Americans.

EMPHATICALLY POSITIVE FREEDOM

Fourth, the framers' insistence on the importance of virtue for freedom puts them squarely against much modern thinking in the debate between negative freedom, or freedom from interference, and positive freedom, or freedom for excellence. As we saw in chapter two, the American Revolution was unashamedly a struggle to gain negative freedom. Quite simply, the Declaration of Independence is the grandest and most influential statement of freedom from interference in history. But unlike many modern citizens, the founders did not stop there. They were equally committed to the complementary importance of freedom for excellence. Their aim, as we saw, was liberty and not just independence.

In other words, the founders held that not just individuals but the republic itself had an ongoing interest in the virtue of the citizenry. Private virtue was a public interest, not only for leaders but for everyone, and this was a prime motive in the rise of the common schools and the place of public education. Article III of the Northwest Ordinance, passed by the Confederation Congress and affirmed by the First Congress under the Constitution, stated plainly at the outset: "Religion, morality, and knowledge being necessary to good government and the happiness of mankind, schools and the means of education shall for ever be encouraged."

Does this mean, as some charge, that the framers were smuggling an aristocracy of virtue back into the republic and were therefore undemocratic and fell foul of Tocqueville's accusation that Athens was an "aristocracy of masters"?[51] In a sense, the answer is yes. The republic clearly required leaders and citizens who took virtue seriously, especially at the level of the highest national affairs. In the picture that Cicero used before the Roman Senate, citizens whose character and virtue can be "weighed" are worth more to the republic than citizens who can only be "counted."

But the accusation of an American aristocracy of virtue is miscast. In a democratic republic the size of the United States, the choice is not between an aristocracy and no aristocracy, or between aristocracy and pure democracy. Representative democracy is inevitably aristocratic in one sense, for it chooses the few to represent the many.

Thus as soon as the choice is made for "representative" rather than the "pure" or "complete" democracy of Athens, there will have to be explicit or implicit criteria for the way citizens choose who will represent them. Rule out virtue as a criterion, and something else will take its place—most probably money or fame. Benjamin Rush lamented long ago that America was becoming a "bedollared nation."[52]

As contemporary American politics illustrates all too clearly, the founders' aristocracy of virtue has been well and truly replaced by what the English writer William Cobbett called the worst of all aristocracies—"moneyed aristocracy."[53] Money rather than monarchy and plutocracy rather than theocracy are the chief threats to republicanism today.

Some Americans, such as Mitt Romney, use their mega-wealth to pursue the presidency. Others, such as Bill Clinton, use the presidency to pursue their mega-wealth. But either way, the rule of money in American public life expands in leaps and bounds, so that, like Athens, the United States is becoming an aristocratic commonwealth and, even worse, a full-blooded plutocracy that is increasingly shut off to the moderately wealthy and the poor.

Without virtue, there would be no freedom. Indeed, without virtue there would be no citizens at all, for it takes a certain virtue to transform the private concerns of individuals into the public concerns of citizens willing and able to participate in the common discussion of the common good. In the language of the Athenian democrats, it takes virtue to transform the "idiot" (the purely private person) and the "tribesperson" (the member of a group) into the "citizen." For all these reasons, the framers were as committed to positive freedom as to negative freedom. They were convinced that personal virtue was a public matter for the republic, whatever the private concern for virtue that the individual, the family and the faith community might also have. That freedom requires virtue, then, is the first leg of the golden triangle.

VIRTUE REQUIRES FAITH

If the framers' position on virtue is suspect today and needs to pass through stringent intellectual security checks, how much more so their views on religion. Indeed, they are an open battleground, and all the earlier qualifications about virtue need to be underscored once again, and others added (the founders were not all people of faith; they had very different views of the relationship of religion and public life, for example). Yet the overall evidence for what they argued is again massive and unambiguous, even from some of the more unlikely sources such as Jefferson and Paine: the founders believed that if freedom requires virtue, *virtue in turn requires faith* (of some sort).

"If Men are so wicked as we now see them with Religion," Benjamin Franklin said, "what would they be without it?"[54]

"It is impossible to account for the creation of the universe without the agency of a Supreme Being," George Washington wrote, "and it is impossible to govern the universe without the aid of a Supreme Being."[55]

"We have no government armed with powers capable of contending with human passions unbridled by morality and religion," John Adams wrote. "Avarice, ambition, revenge or gallantry would break the strongest cords of our Constitution as a whale goes through a net. Our Constitution was made only for a moral and religious people. It is wholly inadequate to the government of any other."[56]

"Should our Republic ever forget this fundamental precept of governance," John Jay wrote about the importance of faith for virtue, "men are certain to shed their responsibilities for licentiousness and this great experiment will surely be doomed."[57]

"The only surety for a permanent foundation of virtue is religion," Abigail Adams wrote. "Let this important truth be engraved upon your heart."[58]

"Can the liberties of a nation be thought secure," Thomas Jefferson wrote, "when we have removed their only firm basis, a conviction in the minds of the people, that these liberties are the gift of God? That they are violated but with his wrath? I tremble for my country when I reflect that God is just, and that His justice cannot sleep for ever."[59]

"Is there no virtue among us?" James Madison asked. "If there be not, we are in a wretched situation. No theoretical checks—no form of government can render us secure. To suppose that any form of government can secure liberty or happiness without virtue in the people is a chimerical idea."[60]

"The wise politician," Alexander Hamilton wrote, "knows that morality overthrown (and morality must fall with religion), the terrors of despotism can alone curb the impetuous passions of man, and confine him within the bounds of social duty."[61]

Did this emphasis on religion mean that the framers were arguing for an official "Christian America"? Not at all. Unquestionably most Americans at the time of the revolution were either Christians or from a Christian background, and most American ideas were directly or indirectly rooted in the Jewish and Christian faiths. Thus even Franklin as a freethinker, writing to Ezra Stiles in 1790, made clear that he would never become a Christian, yet stated this: "As to Jesus of Nazareth, my Opinion of whom you particularly desire, I think the System of Morals and his Religion, as he left them to us, the best the World ever saw or is likely to see."[62]

But the historical and statistical importance of the Christian faith in 1776 did not for a moment translate into any official position for the Christian faith or for any notion of a "Christian nation." Joel Barlow, who negotiated the Treaty of Tripoli with the Pasha in 1796, may have been a deist with little sympathy for the Christian faith, but his famous clause to the treaty caused little stir at the time: "As the government of the United States of America is not in any sense founded on the Christian religion."[63]

Beyond that untypically bald statement: the First Amendment, on the one hand, barred any official national establishment of religion, and over the next decades the States slowly came into line until the last establishment had gone. On the other hand, many of the framers, like President Eisenhower in the 1950s, spoke of religion in generic rather than specific terms, and they advocated religion only for secular or utilitarian reasons that the Romans understood well and on which Edward Gibbon commented famously. Religion, at the very least, was the sole force capable of fostering the virtue and restraining the vice necessary for the health of the republic.

Significantly, Franklin, for example, went on from the quotation above to underscore that he was interested in "the fundamental Principles of all sound Religion," which he found in many sects and faiths. And what concerned Washington in his "Farewell Address" was not religious orthodoxy itself but the eminently practical point that "true religion and good morals are the only solid foundations of public liberty and happiness."[64] For his part, Jefferson greatly preferred Unitarianism to the Christian faith, and eagerly looked forward to its expected triumph over traditional faith, but his interest was not in polemical issues. "Both religions," he wrote, "make honest men, and that is the only point society has any authority to look to."[65]

WHAT ABOUT ATHEISTS?

Did this emphasis on religion mean that the framers did not grant freedom of conscience to atheists or that they thought atheists would not be good citizens? Again, emphatically not. In addition to the First Amendment, the Constitution itself required that there be no religious test for office in the United States. Properly speaking, atheism (or secularism as a practical form of atheism) is itself a worldview or form of faith, though expressly naturalistic and non-supernatural. But regardless of philosophical niceties, the framers were emphatic that the right of freedom of conscience, or religious liberty, was absolute, unconditional and a matter of equality for all.

As early as 1644, Roger Williams had staked out the radical position in "The Bloudy Tenent of Persecution" that freedom of conscience, or "soul freedom," meant "a permission of the most paganish, Jewish, Turkish, or anti-Christian consciences and worships, be granted to all men in all nations and countries."[66] A century and a half later, the same note of universality and equality rings out clearly in 1785 in Madison's "Memorial and Remonstrance": "Above all are they to be considered as retaining an 'equal to the free exercise of Religion according to the dictates of conscience.'"[67] John Adams wrote unequivocally to his son, "Government has no Right to hurt a hair of the head of an Atheist for his Opinions."[68]

It must be added, however, that like Voltaire and other Enlightenment philosophers who disdained religion, the founders were less sanguine about the consequences of a government of atheists or a society of atheists. "It would be better far," John Adams wrote, "to turn back to the gods of the Greeks than to endure a government of atheists."

Secularists, of course, are free to counter the founders' misgivings by demonstrating their capacity to build an enduring, nationwide foundation for the virtues needed for the American republic on entirely secular grounds, grounds that need no place at all for religious beliefs. Thoughtful atheists, such as Christopher Hitchens, have stated this claim boldly in theory, but its challenge remains to be picked up in practice. The plain fact is that no free and lasting civilization anywhere in history has so far been built on atheist foundations. At the very least, it would be a welcome change for secularists to shift from their strident attacks on religiously based virtues to building their own replacements and attempting to persuade a majority of their fellow citizens of their merits.

What are we to make of the founders' misgivings about a society of atheists? Is it an inconsistency or a form of hypocrisy or perhaps even an egregious contradiction like their views of slavery? Were they simply reacting to the excesses of the French Revolution? There was certainly an element of the latter. Washington referred delicately in his "Farewell Address" to the malign influence of "refined education on minds of peculiar structure," and Hamilton blasted the

French radicals more openly. "The attempt by the rulers of a nation to destroy all religious opinion, and pervert a whole people to Atheism," he wrote, "is a phenomenon of profligacy reserved to consummate the infamy of the unbridled reformers of France!"[69] But the founders' position was far more thoughtful than just a reaction. They were convinced that only faiths that (in modern parlance) were thick rather than thin would have the power to promote and protect virtue. After all, raise such questions as "Why be virtuous?" "What is virtue?" and "What happens if someone is not virtuous?" and anyone can see the faiths have more to say about the inspiration, content and sanctions for virtue than any other form of human thought—and that is certainly so for the overwhelming majority of people outside the circles of higher education.

Needless to say, individual atheists and secularists can be virtuous too—far more so in some cases than many religious believers. But the political question is whether atheism and secularism can provide a sufficient foundation to foster the needed virtues of the wider citizenry over the course of the running generations. This task waits to be demonstrated.

CYNICAL OR UTILITARIAN?

The founders' stress on the need for faith can be expressed cynically, and Gibbon is often quoted for his famous comment on the Roman attitude toward religion. Voltaire scornfully dismissed religion for "respectable people" like himself and his friends, though he advocated it for the rest: "I want my lawyer, my tailor, my servants, even my wife to believe in God, because it means that I shall be cheated and robbed and cuckolded less often."[70] But the evidence from the American founders suggests that they were utilitarian rather than cynical. They sincerely believed that, even if they themselves did not claim a faith, it would take faith to do the job of shaping the virtue needed to promote and protect republican freedom.

For some of the framers, such a view was unquestionably utilitarian—and somewhat cynical. But it was not necessarily hypocritical. And it was this functional appreciation of faith that lay behind several incidents for which the framers have been charged with hypocrisy—for instance, the story Ethan Allen told of a friend meeting President Jefferson on his way to church one Sunday "with his large red prayer book under his arm," and exchanging greetings.

"Which way are you walking, Mr. Jefferson?" the friend asked.

"To church, Sir," the president replied.

"You going to church, Mr. J. You do not believe a word in it."

"Sir," said Mr. Jefferson, "no nation has ever yet existed or been governed without religion. Nor can be. The Christian religion is the best religion that has ever been given to man and I as Chief Magistrate of this nation am bound to give it the sanction of my example. Good morning, Sir."[71]

Jefferson's example is instructive. In two important areas, there was a striking gap between his private and public views—over slavery and over religion in public life. In the case of slavery, it is hard not to conclude that the writer of the Declaration of Independence was hypocritical. He owned more than three hundred slaves in his lifetime; he had more when he died than when he wrote the Declaration. And he imported slaves into France, where he knew slavery was illegal and not customary as it was in Virginia. But beyond his vested interest in his own slaves, there was always his anguish over the unavoidable dilemma he saw: the slaves' freedom would endanger America's freedom. In his own words, he was caught as he admitted between "justice in one scale, and self-preservation in the other."[72]

In the case of religion in public life, Jefferson was probably not so much hypocritical or anguished as utilitarian and savvy. He was a deist who undoubtedly loathed organized religion and serious theology of all kinds—Protestant, Catholic and Jewish. He believed the Christian faith had been seriously corrupted and would soon be replaced by Unitarianism, and he was a church-state separationist who fiercely defended his "wall of separation." Yet as the conversation with Ethan Allen shows, whether Jefferson was two-faced or simply utilitarian, there is no question that he also believed that freedom requires virtue, and virtue faith, and that he as chief magistrate must support certain public expressions of faith.

FAITH REQUIRES FREEDOM

Needless to say, the third leg of the golden triangle is the most radical, and if the first two legs challenge the unexamined assumptions of many liberals today, the third does the same for many conservatives: faith requires freedom.

Nothing, absolutely nothing in the American experiment is more revolutionary, unique and decisive than the first sixteen words of the First Amendment that are the "Religious Liberty Clauses." At one stroke, what Marx called "the flowers on the chains" and Lord Acton the "gilded crutch of absolutism" was stripped away.[73] The persecution that Roger Williams called "spiritual rape" and a "soul yoke" and that Lord Acton called "spiritual murder" was prohibited.[74] The burden of centuries of oppression was lifted; what Williams lamented as "the rivers of civil blood" spilled by faulty relations between religion and government were staunched; and faith was put on its free and fundamental human footing as "soul freedom"—Williams's term for what was a matter of individual conscience and uncoerced freedom. The Williamsburg Charter, a celebration of the genius of the First Amendment on the occasion of its two hundredth anniversary, summarized the public aspect of this stunning achievement:

> No longer can sword, purse, and sacred mantle be equated. Now, the government is barred from using religion's mantle to become a confessional State, and from allowing religion to use the government's sword and purse to become a coercing Church. In this new order, the freedom of the government

from religious control and the freedom of religion from government control are a double guarantee of the protection of rights. No faith is preferred or prohibited, for where there is no state-definable orthodoxy, there can be no state-definable heresy.[75]

The First Amendment was of course no bolt out of the blue. It was the crowning achievement of the long, slow, tortuous path to religious liberty that grew out of the horrors of the Wars of Religion and the daring bravery of thinkers such as Roger Williams, William Penn, John Leland, Isaac Backus, George Mason, Thomas Jefferson, James Madison, the Culpeper Baptists and many others.

Many of the great peaks of the story of religious freedom and many of the greatest protagonists of religious liberty lie in the terrain of American history. In the "argument between friends," for example, the maverick dissenter Roger Williams clashed with the orthodox John Cotton of Boston in challenging the notion of "the uniformity of religion in a civil state" and the "doctrine of persecution" that inevitably accompanied it. This pernicious doctrine, he said, "is proved guilty of all the blood of the souls crying for vengeance under the altar." In its place, he asserted, "it is the will and command of God that . . . a permission of the most paganish, Jewish, Turkish, or anti-Christian consciences and worships, be granted to all men in all countries: and that they are only to be fought against with that sword which is only (in soul matters) able to conquer, to wit, the sword of God's spirit, the Word of God."[76]

Almost like an echo, Madison rang out the same themes in his "Memorial and Remonstrance" protesting against Patrick Henry's proposal to levy a religion tax that everybody could earmark for the church of his or her choice. No, the little man with the quiet voice protested, hammering home point after point with precision as well as force that this was absolutely wrong and there was a better way. Among the highlights of Madison's historic protest are the following:

First, the principle of religious liberty, or freedom of conscience, is foundational and inviolable: "We hold it for a fundamental and undeniable truth, 'that Religion or the duty which we owe to our Creator and the manner of discharging it, can be directed only by reason and conviction, not by force or violence.' The Religion then of every man must be left to the conviction and conscience of every man; and it is the right of every man to exercise it as these may dictate. . . . This right is in its nature an unalienable right."[77]

Second, understanding that the flower is present in the seed and the greatest problems start with the smallest beginnings, "it is proper to take alarm at the first experiment on our liberties." Even a minute tax of three-pence on behalf of religion should be enough to sound the alarm: "Distant as it may be in its present form from the Inquisition, it differs from it only in degree."

Third, the principle that rights are both inalienable and equal operates like the Golden Rule for religious liberty, "while we assert for ourselves a freedom to embrace, to profess and to observe the Religion which we believe to be of divine origin, we cannot deny an equal freedom to those whose minds have not yet yielded to the evidence which has convinced us."

Fourth, it is both wrong and foolish to think "that the Civil Magistrate is a competent judge of Religious truth; or that he may employ Religion as an engine of Civil policy." (Or as Pastor John Leland wrote tartly, "If government can answer for individuals on the day of judgment, let men be controlled by it in religious matters; otherwise let men be free."[78])

Fifth, the Christian faith needs no government support. To say that it does is "a contradiction to the Christian Religion itself; for every page of it disavows a dependence on the powers of this world."

Sixth, establishing religion is disastrous for the church. "What have been its fruit? More or less in all places, pride and indolence in the Clergy; ignorance and servility in the laity; in both, superstition, bigotry, and persecution."

Seventh, established religions are bad for civil government. "In some instances they have been seen to erect a spiritual tyranny on the ruins of Civil authority; in many instances they have been seen upholding the thrones of political tyranny; in no instances have they been seen the guardians of the liberties of the people."

Eighth, any establishment of religion departs from the generous American policy of "offering asylum to the persecuted and oppressed of every Nation and Religion" and thus lights "a Beacon on our coasts warning [the asylum seeker] to seek some other haven, where liberty and philanthropy in their due extent may offer a more certain repose from his troubles."

Ninth, failure to guarantee religious liberty for all destroys the "moderation and harmony" of "the true remedy" that the United States has brought to an issue that elsewhere has spilt "torrents of blood."

All these principles are as fresh today as when Madison wrote them. Freedom of conscience, for example, is the best single antidote to the radical extremism of certain Muslims, as it is to the state-favored secularism of the European Union and as it is to the illiberalism of American legal secularism. Coercion and compulsion from one side and exclusion from the public square from the other contradict conscience, and therefore freedom, at its core.

Without coming to grips with freedom of conscience, Islam cannot modernize peacefully, Europe cannot advance freely and America will never fulfill the promise of its great experiment in freedom. The present liberal reliance on such purely negative notions as hate speech and hate crimes is both inadequate and foolish, and can even be dangerous. Without acknowledging the cornerstone place of religious liberty, Europe will not be able to accommodate both liberty and cultural diversity; Muslims will not be able to maintain the integrity of their own faith under the conditions of modernity, let alone learn to live peacefully with others; and America will never create the truly civil and cosmopolitan public square that the world requires today.

But Madison's principles challenge conservatives and Christians too. No conservative or Christian who applies the golden rule set out by Madison—more properly, by Jesus of Nazareth and other religious leaders—to issues such as prayer in public schools can argue for it as the religious right has done. And no Christian who appreciates the importance of Madison's insistence on faith communities trusting in God rather than Caesar can fail to have reservations about "faith-based initiatives" in the form in which they were first promoted.

Many of the attacks on the faith-based initiatives have been unfair. Thomas Friedman, a *New York Times* reporter, for instance, lambasted a "faith-based" president for launching "a faith-based war in Iraq, on the basis of faith-based intelligence, with a faith-based plan for Iraqi reconstruction."[79] Yet Friedman supported the war, and the "faith" at fault in Iraq was not one of the faiths aided by the faith-based initiatives but the utopian faith in democracy of the neoconservatives.

Supporters have praised the faith-based initiatives as equal treatment for secular and religious providers, while critics have generally focused on practical flaws in the approach. The initiatives have been attacked as a form of cronyism (with the new grants going mainly to religious groups that involve the president's friends and supporters). It is said too they will inevitably lead to secularizing religious organizations, which will have to cut out many of their distinctively religious practices to qualify for the government grant (faith-based organizations become secular, as one analyst puts it, while secular organizations stay secular). And above all, the faith-based initiatives were doomed to be controversial from the start because they never set out a vision of a civil public square that would guarantee freedom and justice for all. Sure enough, they at once set off another round of culture warring.

But for Christians, the real flaw of the policy is in principle. By inviting churches and other faith communities to accept government money, even so much as a cent, the policy undermines an essential aspect of Christian faith and contradicts a key part of American voluntarism. What was constitutionally controversial became entangled with what was spiritually unwise. As Madison wrote to Edward Livingston, "an alliance or coalition between Government and religion cannot be too carefully guarded against . . . religion and government will exist in greater purity, without (rather) than with the aid of government." Churches cannot have their cake and eat it too. If they want the government to keep its hands off the church, they should keep their own noses out of the government trough.

Christians who support the faith-based initiatives with fervor forget the lessons of history and the important paradox expressed by Peter Berger: "The worldly contribution of religion remains possible only if religion itself remains other-worldly."[80] In other words, Christian dependency is as much a problem as government demands. Referring to the earliest and most fateful dependence of the church on state support, Rodney Stark writes, "Christianity might have been far better served had Constantine's faith been pretended. For, in doing his best to serve Christianity, Constantine destroyed its most vital aspect: *its dependence on mass voluntarism.*"[81]

This particular issue has been dealt with by others and in greater depth, so I need not pursue it further.[82] What matters here is the revolutionary character of the framers' idea of religious liberty, as well as their clear understanding that it was an integral part of their vision of sustaining freedom. The revolutionaries in France and strict separationists in America today have a concept of *laicite*, or the strictest separation of church and state, which is purely reactionary and has no positive place for freedom of conscience at all. The First Amendment, by contrast, is truly about liberty, though "liberty for all" is seen as the best remedy for countering extremism by some, and as always the good of the republic is not far away. "Rival sects, with equal rights," Madison underscored, "exercise mutual censorships in favor of good morals."[83]

In 1792, Madison captured the originality of what they had attempted in creating the Constitution: "In Europe, charters of liberty have been granted by power. America has set the example and France has followed it, of charters of power granted by liberty."[84] Whether he would have still included the French ten years later is another question. But his point remains, as does its challenge.

The liberty of the American republic is not self-sustaining, and it needs a safeguard beyond that of the Constitution and its separation of powers. But what does it take to turn parchment barriers into living bulwarks? What is the catalyst that can bond together the external laws of the Constitution with the internal commitments and duties of citizens—rulers no less than ruled? The framers' answer was to understand, cultivate and transmit the golden triangle of liberty, and thus the habits of the heart that sustained the citizens and the republic alike.

That is true liberal education, or *paideia*. There is simply no schooling and no apprenticeship that is more challenging yet more fruitful than that. Freedom requires virtue, which in turn requires faith of some sort, which in turn requires freedom. Only so can a free people hope to remain "free always." For Americans must never forget: all who aspire to be like Rome in their beginnings must avoid being like Rome at their ending. Rome and its republic fell, and so too will the American republic—unless . . .

5

THE COMPLETEST
REVOLUTION OF ALL

ONE OF THE DELIGHTS OF AMERICA IS THE WAY in which the character of the nation can be captured in the humblest of throwaway remarks. When President Carter gave the Medal of Freedom to Eugene Ormandy, director of the Philadelphia Orchestra, in 1980, the great conductor remarked to a group of reporters: "People always ask me where I was born. I was born at the age of twenty-one, when I arrived in the United States." Earlier in the 1960s, when Admiral Rickover made a visit to his native Poland, a reporter asked him, "Will you visit the town where you were born?" Rickover answered tersely, "What for?"[1]

From their nation's very beginning, and largely because of its beginnings, Americans have a pronounced habit of minimizing continuity and exaggerating change. This can be seen in a whole range of things. Some are trivial, such as claims for "all-new" television programs and "miracle" weight-loss programs. Some are more consequential, such as glowing accounts of complete transformation through the alchemy of American immigration. Moving from the Old World to the New, it was said, new arrivals in America completed a revolutionary threefold shift: from being members of a group to being individuals, from being defined by blood ties to being defined by beliefs and from an orientation toward the past to an orientation toward the future.

To be sure, each of these shifts was substantial and important, both for the new arrivals and for America. Historians have debated about how complete the change was and what its costs were when it was complete. But beyond question, all such shifts have been significantly lessened today. Such factors as the power of roots, the place of identity politics, the ease of transportation and communication, and the close proximity of some of the countries of origin, such as Mexico, have blurred the old claims beyond recognition. Complete change in the old way is therefore no longer viewed as desirable or possible.

One age-old contrast, however, remains an issue for Americans: the contrast between Europe and the United States. It is a prosaic fact, and not a European conceit, that Europe is the fountainhead of the greater part of American culture and the birthplace of most of the ancestors of the Americans who shaped the founding and rise of America. At the same time, Europe and America have always been two states of mind as much as two places on a map. To be American has always been to be ex-European, and this non-Europeanness has been an important foil to Americanness, even where the differences are mythical and hard to pin down.

Put differently, Europeanness became a blank sheet on which all that was inadmissible and undesirable to Americans could be posted and attacked as European—just as today Americanism serves as the blank sheet on which the rest of the world can vent its anger and frustration at the world's lead society.

But what is the relationship of Europe and America now? Some argue that America is being "Europeanized," as H. L. Mencken charged earlier and critics of America's growing secularity say today. Others claim with equal vigor that Europe is being "Americanized" and point to the spread of American popular culture. (The French famously described the introduction of Disneyland to Paris as a "cultural Chernobyl.") Still others argue that, though the original differences between them have lessened and the mythical ones have outgrown their usefulness, Europe and the United States are beginning to go in two very different directions so that there is no longer any identifiable West, or at least any united West.

Jürgen Habermas, the eminent European philosopher, argues that we are seeing a "divided West," with Europe moving toward a cosmopolitan global vision and the United States pressing toward its own vision of "hegemonic liberalism."[2] Robert Kagan claims that "Americans are from Mars and Europeans are from Venus."[3] Reeling from a century of their own virulent nationalisms, disastrous world wars and indescribable evils such as the Nazi death camps, Europeans are relapsing into an irresponsible, near-utopian pacifism, while sheltering under the shield of American arms.

Addressing the same gap from a different direction, George Weigel has analyzed the difference as between "the Cube and the Cathedral"—between Francois Mitterand's Grand Arche, representing the hard-edged rationality of French secularism, and the Cathedral of Notre Dame, representing America's far greater openness to the place of religion in national life.[4]

For both Kagan and Weigel, the United States now has a "Europe problem" that is quite different from earlier American problems with Europe. In the past, there was a simple solution to any problem Europe represented: leave Europe and become an American. Today, however, Europe's divergent direction is seen as a problem for the future of the United States itself, either militarily in the case of Europe's Venus-like mood or culturally in Europe's preference for the Cube over the Cathedral.

Cosmopolitan globalism versus hegemonic liberalism, Venus versus Mars, the Cube versus the Cathedral, the first of the transnationalizing communities versus the greatest of the current world's nation-states—such arguments bounce back and forth, but one factor critical to our discussion of sustainable freedom must not be lost in the hubbub. From the perspective of some of the keenest European admirers of America, there is a key difference between Europe and the United States that could one day prove to be America's Achilles' heel: unlike Europe, America enjoys such freedom and mobility that it relies more than it realizes on the bonding constraints of its faiths and its moral standards. If these restraints were to fail, the consequences could be far greater in America than they would be in Europe.

Americans tend to snort when this point is raised—Europeans, they say, are notoriously less moral than Americans. But they miss the point. The average European is certainly more secular and far less morally concerned than the average American, though Europeans find American obsession over the private lives of politicians incomprehensible and believe that European concern for social responsibility over issues such as poverty, human rights and the environment is just as ethical as American concerns for life and marriage. But that said, Europe still has two things that the United States increasingly lacks: tradition and close-knit living situations. While these last, they together provide some restraint on freedom in the absence of faith and moral standards.

Put differently, America's very distinctiveness highlights its potential dilemma. The United States is vulnerable to a crisis of cultural authority precisely because it is a nation by intention and by ideas, and it relies so deeply on them. And if Tocqueville was correct that in America religion is "the first of the political institutions," then either the weakening or the repression of religion in America will be of first importance. "How can society fail to perish if, while the political bond is relaxed, the moral bond is not drawn tight?"[5] As with any nation, the very principles by which America arose will determine the pathologies by which America will decline.

Lord James Bryce was Queen Victoria's ambassador to Washington and an astute foreign observer second only to Tocqueville.

Pondering the significance of religion to America, he remarked that he was "startled by the thought of what might befall this huge yet delicate fabric of laws and commerce and social institutions were the foundation [of religion] it has rested on to crumble away." America, he concluded soberly, is "the country in which the loss of faith in the invisible might produce *the completest revolution*, because it is the country where men have been least wont to revere anything in the visible world."[6]

The English journalist G. K. Chesterton made a similar point after his tour of the United States in 1921. He was "no Futurist," he said, but there were certain things about America's future that anyone who thought carefully could see with little or no clairvoyance. American democracy had been grounded in convictions that were essentially religious, so those convictions could not decay or be rejected with impunity. American democracy would either keep its basis and remain democratic, or it would lose its basis and become "wildly and wickedly undemocratic." Whichever way history went, he concluded, some "ultimate test will come."[7]

THE EXPERIMENT NEVER ENDS

Can freedom last forever, as the founders believed? Are Americans sustaining freedom today in a manner that makes it likely to endure strongly for the next generations? These questions require answering at two levels. The first and most important level (and the theme of this chapter) is domestic. After two and a third centuries, what is the condition of American freedom at home? The second level is the international level. What is the condition of American freedom that is demonstrated by American actions abroad (the theme of the next chapter)?

Some people doubt the value of raising such questions. So it is important to recognize that the need for vigilance was a corollary of the open-endedness of the American experiment from the beginning. In John Winthrop's terms mentioned earlier, America would either be "a city upon a hill" or it would become "a story and a by-word throughout the world." But unlike most experiments, the American experiment will continue to be open-ended to the end. It is, after all, an experiment to see whether a free people can remain free *forever*.

I have met many Americans who reject both Washington's term "the great experiment" and any stress on perpetual open-endedness. "The growth and success of the United States was never in doubt," one conservative senator asserted to me. "They were America's destiny, and a mark of the sure hand of God on us in blessing." "Open-ended?" a more liberal journalist asked. "Why do you talk about an open-ended experiment when people are lining up around the block to get in? The experiment is a clear and resounding success."

Such objections would certainly hold for the first two parts of establishing a free republic. In terms of *winning* and *ordering* freedom, the American experiment has been a resounding success, and the book can be closed on those two issues. The founding generation dared, the founding generation succeeded, and its glory will never be dimmed. But by its very nature, present success is no answer to the potential challenges of *sustaining* freedom, and the book on the third task must be kept open and watched closely, generation by generation.

At the heart of the American experiment, two things will remain open-ended forever. The first is the nature of freedom itself. Freedom never lasts forever, because its very vitality is built on a combination of elements that are dynamic, difficult to hold together and easy to corrupt. As history shows, freedom repeatedly loses its vigor and undermines itself.

Sometimes freedom collapses into a freedom-destroying license, especially when it loses its crucial self-restraint. At other times freedom suffers a sclerotic hardening because of a desire for false security and an aversion to taking risks (ironically the land of the free now has achieved levels of security and surveillance that would be the envy of most dictators). And sometimes freedom becomes twisted into hypocrisy as freedom conducts itself in ways through which it becomes the loser (which Niall Ferguson describes as the American paradox of "dictating democracy, of enforcing freedom, of extorting emancipation").[8]

Each of these specters has risen in American history before, and each became a growing menace after 9/11—not least because American presidents resort to a rationale that is prone to self-deception, that is, whatever is done in the name of freedom must automatically be right and good.

A DEMOCRATIC GAMBLE

The second open-ended feature of the American experiment lies in the gamble at the heart of democratic freedom. It can be expressed like this: Constitutionally speaking, there is no limit to what anyone in America can believe, though culturally speaking, there is an obvious limit. On the one hand, particular beliefs and opinions might arise that would undermine the foundations of the American experiment itself. On the other hand, the whole way of holding any beliefs could be undermined, either through tolerating all beliefs so indiscriminately that tolerance slumps into indifference or through obstructing all beliefs so strictly that they cannot exert any influence on public life.

Fortunately, Americans with openly subversive beliefs have little political power today—for example, Muslim radicals who advocate replacing the Constitution with a Caliphate, or Christian Reconstructionists who talk of playing the pluralistic game only to put the enemies of God out of the game (their hardball equivalent of the Middle Eastern tactic of "one man, one vote, one time"). Neither position is currently a serious menace, except in the fevered nightmares of their critics, but the social logic of their position should always be borne in mind.

Conversely, those who represent a weak form of the danger are more numerous and influential—for example, views that undermine key features of the American experiment such as human rights and the dignity of human persons. The founders were not unaware of this possibility. In his "Discourses on Davila," John Adams speculated on just such views arising, and did so in words that come uncannily close to views that are widespread in postmodern discussion today.

Is there a possibility that the government of nations may fall into the hands of men who teach the most disconsolate of all creeds, that men are but fireflies and that this *all* is without a father? Is this the way to make man, as man, an object of respect? Or is it to make murder itself as indifferent as shooting a plover, and the extermination of the Rohilla nation as innocent as the swallowing of mites on a morsel of cheese?[9]

For the founders, the way to resolve this tension between unlimited constitutional freedom and unquestioned cultural dangers was through tough, robust, civil, open deliberation and debate. If the people's eventual decisions were deliberated and debated in this way, they would be wiser and more acceptable; and in the process, the inadequacies of error could be exposed and challenged. In his first inaugural address, Jefferson declared that "error of opinion may be tolerated where reason is left free to combat it."[10]

But therein lies the democratic gamble. The best, most true, most human, most just, most liberating and most beautiful views must prevail in open debate in generation after generation. If they do not, the American experiment will fail in the end, especially if there is no agreement as to whether there is any such thing as truth underlying the debates.

Jefferson quoted the old Irish maxim "Truth is great and shall prevail." His confidence in truth would still be shared today by Jews and Christians, among others. But it would be widely dismissed by many others—by postmodernists as wrong-headed, by evolutionary naturalists as pious fiction and by political consultants as old-fashioned and naive. To the first group, there is no such thing as truth—knowledge is simply power. To the second, truth has no ultimate status, and deception may hold the winning cards in the struggle for the survival of the fittest. And to the third, truth has nothing to do with the winning formulae of negative advertising. In short, in America today, truth itself, rather than particular claims to truth, is in question—and the political significance of that needs to be debated too.

Jefferson is famous for the bravado in which he expressed to the French the vital distinction between beliefs and behavior. "The legitimate powers of government extend to such acts only as are injurious to others. But it does me no injury for my neighbor to say that there are twenty gods, or no God. It neither picks my pocket nor breaks my leg."[11]

But ideas do have consequences, very real consequences. There is unquestionably a crucial difference between freedom of beliefs and freedom of behavior, and only the former is absolute. But many people then, and many now, would also argue that the distinction must never become a divorce, for the link between belief and behavior is sure and consequential. Words are not sticks and stones that break our bones, but in the long run they are even more powerful.

Take the great issue behind the Civil War: were the African-American slaves full humans or were they three-fifths humans? The answer to that question was not semantic. It was enough to divide America, and rightly though devastatingly so.

Or take one of the two great issues at stake in the culture wars now. What if either pro-life beliefs or pro-choice beliefs were to prevail decisively one day? Both sides would argue that the result would be decisive—increased back-alley abortions and decreased freedom for women, as one side sees it; or millions more humans and American citizens alive and well, as the other side sees it. Such beliefs pick no pockets and break no legs. But they do more: they decide life and death—literally—for millions of Americans.

Put these open-ended features of the American experiment together, and they highlight the monumental wager behind democracy in general and the American republic in particular. Complacency is out of order. Far better the wry modesty of Churchill's remark about democracy as "the worst system there is, except for all the others." Freedom has been won and freedom has been ordered, but when it comes to sustaining freedom, the jury is still out. Unless America can be the first to buck history, history's foregone conclusion is that American freedom will go the way of all other political systems. But that, of course, is the issue now at stake, and any who reject the founders' solution to the challenge must be all the clearer about their own.

THE ALIENATION OF LEADERS

In the third chapter, I set out the three classical menaces to freedom, which the framers endeavored to resist in establishing a free society that could remain free. Let me now add to that by discussing three contemporary menaces to sustainable freedom, the last of which is the most lethal because it attacks the very nature of freedom itself.

The first contemporary menace comes from the fact that many American leaders, particularly those who shape opinion, show a marked alienation from the ideas and core assumptions of the American founders—and particularly from the founders' notion of how freedom can be sustained.

For most people, the reason for the alienation is simply benign neglect. This is especially the case for those who unthinkingly accept the notion that the Constitution is all that matters. With many, this neglect is deepened by what Max Weber, and more recently Jürgen Habermas, described as the "tone deafness" and "unmusicality" of elites toward religion—compounded by a general lack of history and justified by fears that use of the past has become a political and partisan football in the culture wars. For others, the neglect has recently been hardened into prejudice through reading the strident, often irrational and highly illiberal tone of such new atheists as Richard Dawkins and Sam Harris.

For yet others, the answer is a deliberate but moderate dismissal of the founders' provisions, deepened perhaps by tone deafness but justified by twentieth-century views. On the one hand are widespread progressive views, supported even by presidents such as Woodrow Wilson, who regarded the Constitution as outgrown ("the old political formulas do not fit the present problems: they read now like documents taken out of a forgotten age"[12]). On the other hand are views of public life, such as the legal secularism that is the product of the convergence between secularism, strict separationism and the liberal vision of proceduralism. According to this view, championed by notable scholars such as John Rawls, faith, character and virtue are a matter of preference and for the private world only. The public square is to be a strictly neutral arena for competing self-interests, an arena where procedures rather than principles are operative.[13]

For a final group, the dismissal of the founders is more extreme and the debunking total. Postmodern radicals, for example, view the founders not as heroic pioneers of freedom with a tragic blind spot, but as dead, white, European, male slave owners whose hypocrisy vitiates their claims about freedom. Not even the Declaration of Independence is exempt. Far from a "promissory note," as Martin Luther King Jr. called it, all such rhetoric of freedom was a screen to mask the power agendas of the founders, so that their stand for freedom is thrown out along with their slavery—bath water, baby and all.

This last position is the most troubling for America and illustrates the sea change in culture that was heralded by Nietzsche in the 1880s but came into its own in France in the 1960s and even later in the United States. Loosely called postmodernism, the revolutionary ideas behind this shift are fiction-directed in the sense that its advocates do not believe in truth or objective moral standards of any kind. Instead, all that was once considered objectively true or right and good is now seen as a cover for power, or some interest or agenda. Everything is therefore relative and socially constructed; nothing is what it appears to be; and the outcome is a giant game of suspicion, skepticism or cynicism.

The eminent sociologist Philip Rieff described this shift as a *kulturkampf* between the forces of the faith-directed culture of Western and American tradition and those of the fiction-directed culture of the postmodernists and the progressives.[14] Not only is such postmodern skepticism unprecedented in history as a basis for a culture, it will be lethal for the American republic—"the most elaborate act of suicide that Western intellectuals have ever staged," Rieff argues.[15]

Whatever the reasons for this alienation of American leaders and however witting or unwitting the choices behind it, the outcome is fateful. It banishes the founders' provisions for sustainable freedom, it raises the practical question of what will replace them, and it disenfranchises the voices of all who still take the founders seriously in their pursuit of the project of democratic freedom.

Plainly, the logic of this alienation is decisive. No great country or civilization will endure if its intellectual leaders and opinion shapers are at odds with what made the country or civilization what it is, particularly in such a wholesale way. Yet that is increasingly the case with a growing number of intellectuals in the United States. The result is not so much "the West versus the rest" as the West versus itself, and the point at issue is central to the future of America.

In the candid admission of a leading liberal and postmodern philosopher, Richard Rorty, although most Americans take pride in their country, "many of the exceptions to this rule are found in colleges and universities, in the academic departments that have become sanctuaries for left-wing views." For all the great deal of good they have done, "there is a problem with this left: it is unpatriotic."[16]

By all means, let the present generation dismiss the founders' provisions. That is their right. But they should do so carefully, and only after understanding what the founders were trying to do. And they should do so only when they are able to offer better solutions to the great questions the founders were addressing. The global era is the grand age of side effects, of unintended consequences and now of the "unknown aftermath" and "the black swan." It is a time when the real consequences of decisions are discovered long after the original decision makers have gone. At the very least, the decision about America's sustainable freedom should be made as responsibly and openly as decisions about America's sustainable growth and sustainable environment.

BREAKDOWN IN THE TRANSMISSION

The second contemporary menace to American freedom lies in a breakdown in the transmission of American values. Both Jefferson and Tocqueville said in different ways that every generation in a democracy is a new people. If this is so, then America's sustainable freedom depends on an ongoing double transmission of American ideals from generation to generation. One essential handover has to take place between the older generation and the younger generation—through public education. The other essential handover has to take place between those who have been in America longer, for few Americans are true natives, and those who are new arrivals—as part of the process of immigration and integration.

To put the point mildly, the last generation has witnessed a series of mounting concerns that call into question America's success in both public education and immigration. Too often, however, the concerns of education and immigration have been discussed separately, and rarely has the focus been on the interests of the republic, as opposed to that of individuals and groups.

On the one hand, America's public schools have long been central to America as keepers of the vestal flame, in Jefferson's words. Their purpose was to provide more than free, universal education for all the children in one community. It was to move beyond instruction in skills to education in character, ideals and loyalties—and thus to be a moral force for character building and nation forming. Above all, the public schools were to be the place where spiritual divisiveness, born of creeds, and social divisiveness, born of class, could be reconciled— in short, they were designed to build the unity that balances the diversity, and so to help keep *E pluribus Unum* a reality and not simply rhetoric. All this would once have been called "liberal education," the cultivation of the habits of the heart required for liberty.

On the other hand, America's assimilation of new arrivals has long been legendary, creating what Emerson called this "asylum of all nations" and "new race." Today, in spite of all its flaws, the American melting pot—or mosaic or kaleidoscope or salad bowl or reverse Babel—stands in shining contrast to clumsy European attempts to grapple with a tide of immigrants without a myth or model of assimilation. (In a characteristic display of European ineptitude, the Dutch recently gave new immigrants to the Netherlands, including Muslims, a video of Dutch life that includes shots of topless bathing.) "No other nation," Prime Minister Margaret Thatcher said in admiration of the United States, "has so successfully combined people of different races and nations within a single culture."

Few today, however, would be satisfied that this vision for education and immigration is being fulfilled, and the consequences for America are becoming plain. It is increasingly easy to become *an American*, but with the dismal quality of civic education, it is increasingly hard to know what it is to be *American*. And in the case of immigration, without citizenship education there can be no real assimilation, especially for those who agree with the radical Muslim maxim of the Egyptian writer Sayyid Qutb and others: a Muslim has no nationality except his belief.

Should this double neglect continue, a fateful test will come. It is true that immigration has made America, but it is equally true that assimilation has made immigration work for Americans. If America should ever entertain immigration without assimilation, the day would soon come when immigration puts its stamp on America even more than the revolution.

I state this concern frankly as a European and a resident alien, knowing that some will still dismiss the concern as protectionist or xenophobic, born of the fear of the stranger and the Other. On the contrary, it is precisely when America's values are strong that Americans can reach out to others with the welcome that they or their forebears themselves received when they first arrived. It is when American identity is clear that it need fear no challenge from the arrival of others, and it is when America's unity is strong that Americans can trust that diversity will be a source of enrichment rather than impoverishment.

THE CORRUPTION OF CUSTOMS

The third contemporary menace to freedom is the deadliest. It lies in another "corruption of customs." Again, the term comes from Polybius, who was Tocqueville's forerunner in stressing the importance of customs or habits of the heart for the maintenance of freedom. Desirable customs, Polybius argued, are those that strengthen freedom. Objectionable customs are those that weaken or undermine it. A corruption of customs, then, matters decisively.

It could be argued that the very fact of the American culture wars is an expression of a deepening corruption of American customs. Many notions that were once self-evident in America and could be taken for granted across a wide spectrum of differences have been blighted beyond recognition. What is life? What is marriage? What is a family? Does character matter in a leader? Is there such a thing as truth? Does any society, does Western civilization and in particular does the American republic need any compelling truths and objective standards? In each case, changes in thinking and living in the past fifty years have reduced these notions to fictions and in the process have changed American customs beyond recognition.

If Rome's baleful experience is anything to go by, the American republic is on the verge of change as significant as Rome's proved to be in the first century—though world history today prevents the fatal shift from republic to empire that Rome experienced, and suggests a sadder, briefer outcome—decline.

America is experiencing corruptions in many areas today, but I would argue that the most important corruption of customs is the corruption of freedom—important because of its centrality to the American republic. Nothing comes closer to the essence of America or to the heart of the founders' notion of sustaining the republic and nothing reveals more accurately the health of the republic today.

To set this claim in context, let me summarize some of what we have seen about freedom in the discussion so far:

First, freedom never lasts because there is a conundrum at its core that is made up of historical, political and moral elements. So far no political system has been able to crack the conundrum and create a truly durable freedom.

Second, there are several foundational ways of understanding freedom—through concepts, such as negative and positive freedom; through texts, such as the Magna Carta and the Declaration of Independence; and through customs and symbols, such as the flag and the Statue of Liberty.

Third, there are several political impulses that form a trio of political imperatives that are essential for human beings—freedom, yes, as President George W. Bush declared repeatedly, but no less importantly, justice and order.

Fourth, there are several characteristic ways in which freedom is eventually undermined—through an excess of freedom that degenerates into license and permissiveness, a desire for false se-

curity that undermines freedom and a way of fighting for
freedom that contradicts and undermines freedom and so ends
in hypocrisy.

Fifth, there are several common claims for freedom that border
on the utopian: that freedom is possible for all, regardless of
culture; that freedom is always for the good; and that freedom can
end tyranny on the earth and last forever.

All these points form the backdrop to a stunning fact. At their
core, the American culture wars are America's second freedom war,
a struggle for the soul of American culture that is a deep and important clash between two rival understandings of freedom. On one
side are traditional views of freedom, once grounded more specifi-
cally in Jewish and Christian views, which are locked in battle with
modern, secularist views of freedom, championed as progressive.

"Freedom war" was Lincoln's term for the Civil War, for as he said
in 1864, "We all declare for liberty, but in using the same *word*, we do
not all mean the same *thing*."[17] At this juncture of American history,
the outcome of the second freedom war could well decide the success
or failure of the American experiment. Beyond any doubt, the depth
of the divisions will strain the bonds of civility to the breaking point
and demonstrate to the world the health or otherwise of the American
experiment today. For today's "new new order" of freedom is one that
relegates the founders' new order (the *novus ordo seclorum*) into
being the old order that is fought against.

To assess this second freedom war, we have to go back earlier than
most people do and look further ahead than most do. And a word of
warning is in order. As in any culture war, the two sides view each
other as extremes and therefore trade insults over evils and excesses.
It is as if all Christian history is seen through the twin lenses of the
Crusades and the Inquisition, and all secularism through the prism
of Soviet repressions and the stridency of the new atheists.

And not only that. The traditionalist forces, who previously were the dominant majority, are always tempted to resent the loss of their former power, whereas their secularist victors always appear to be jumpy despite their success. Far from being assured in their purported triumph, they are haunted by the thought of any hint of the former regime returning. When the unspoken resentments of the one meet the unacknowledged insecurities of the other, rancor is guaranteed.

Plainly this situation does not make for easy conversation. Yet the issues that divide the camps are crucial for freedom, and they need to be debated and decided if freedom is to be sustained—all within the bounds of robust, tough-minded civility. Consider the very different understandings of freedom that are in conflict between the two sides.

FREEDOM AS A GIFT

The traditional, or Jewish and Christian, way of freedom, stands staunchly on one side of the culture wars. Once unrivalled and sufficient by itself in the Western world, it is supported now by many other religions and stems from a completely different moral vision and way of life from the modern, secularist view. Indeed, it rejects the latter's freedom as a delusion that ends in disappointment and bondage. There are three key features of the traditional view, all of which are straightforward and consequential.

First, the Jewish and Christian way of freedom views freedom as a gift, along with the gift of life itself. From this perspective, it is both wrong and foolish to believe that we humans make ourselves and that life is ours to choose and control. For a start, we are not so much individual specimens of generic humanity as persons made in the image of God, persons who are expressions of different cultures that have brought us into being and shaped us.

We did not choose to be. From our parents to our genes to the color of our eyes and the day and place of our birth, we are dependent on the choices of others; and we grow up with a greater or lesser dependence on our relatives, our teachers, our neighborhoods, our countries, our history and our friends. In short, we are not self-created but creatures of our various cultures, and finally we are human beings who are made in the image of God and who live truly and inescapably "under God."

"What do you have that you did not receive?" Paul of Tarsus asked his readers in Corinth (1 Corinthians 4:7). For most people, the answer to his question unleashes a tidal wave of gratitude and indebtedness that makes thanksgiving a way of life rather than simply an annual holiday. As Rabbi Abraham Joshua Heschel wrote, "I have not brought my being into being. Nor was I thrown into being. My being is obeying the saying, 'Let there be!'"[18] This indeed was the lesson into which Tocqueville condensed the whole of his political thought: "There is nothing less independent than a free citizen."[19]

This view is decisively different from the secularist view. Man made only in the image of Man loses his and her inviolability, for dignity that is self-created is weaker than dignity that is conferred. Mere existence does not add up to human dignity. After all, animals exist and things exist, yet neither is inviolable. Only if humans are made in the image of God—may they be physically and mentally handicapped, socially degraded or educationally deprived—can they always and irrevocably have a precious and inalienable dignity that none may abrogate or harm. *Freedom in this sense is the independence of the dependent and the responsibility of the grateful.*

FREEDOM AS RELATIONSHIP

Second, the Jewish and Christian way of freedom views freedom, as life itself, as a matter of relationship. Whereas an *individual* (from the Latin *individuum*) is an ultimately indivisible minimum, or atom, a person is a person *only in relationship*. It is not that we are bound by the others in our lives, such as our families, friends and neighbors. Rather, it is that we humans become individual people only in relationship with others. We grow and mature only in a rich field of person-to-person interactions with others. A South African proverb says it all: "A person becomes a person through other persons."

Equally, we only grow in character as we become free people who keep our covenant promises in relationship to others. And we only gain our identities and become our names as we grow trustworthy in those relationships—above all, in our relationship with God, whose call in our individual lives is the creative, constitutive event that is our personal equivalent of creation for the universe itself.

In short, freedom assumes and requires covenant, just as covenant assumes and requires freedom. In the Jewish and Christian view, life is not just about us, and we are always beholden to more than ourselves. On the one hand, we are members of communities-in-space. We prize what Charles Taylor calls "essentially together-goods," actions and experiences such as conversation, making love, friendship, dancing and democratic self-government, which in their very essence are "lived and enjoyed together." They make no sense alone, and recognizing this is to see "the fullness of human life as something that happens between people rather than within each one."[20]

On the other hand, we humans are also members of communities-in-time. We who are alive owe our patrimony to those who have gone before us, just as our legacy will be the patrimony of those who come after us. To broaden Burke's view of the state, human life is a partnership, not only between those who are living, but between those who are living, those who are dead and those who are yet to be born—and all of us together under God.

"No man is an island," John Donne wrote famously. Nor are we Robinson Crusoes, each of us a castaway marooned on our own social island. The trouble today, however, is that in the advanced modern world, the bonding of institutions, from marriage to neighborhoods to political parties, is melting faster than polar ice caps, and relationships are ever more atomized, virtual and a matter of temporary convenience rather than lasting covenant.

As a result, the United States is becoming a vast culture of singles and loners, whether unmarried singles or previously married singles. Many individuals have been reduced to what French novelist Michel Houellebecq has called the "elementary particles," or atoms of humanity.[21] Life according to this view is for lone rangers and solo operators, virtuosi of the self for whom "It is all about me" and because "I am worth it." The result is not freedom so much as narcissism, loneliness and alienation. America more and more resembles Heartbreak Hotel, the lodging house of loners.

Were it not for the ever-changing new offers of sensational magazine covers, the bursting supermarket of self-help philosophies and newfangled pop-counseling recipes, the chasm between the freedoms Americans are promised and the reality they come to find would be seen for what it is: a frustration gap, fueled by the mismatch between modern promises and modern disappointments.

"You can be whatever you want to be," Americans are told endlessly. Yet the absurdity of the promise is equaled only by the abjectness of the failure of the outcome—though few are forced to notice because they are already moving on to the new-new offers on the next horizon.

In the traditional Jewish and Christian view, by contrast, there is no greater folly than the masterless self, no greater sadness than the individual for whom relationships have been reduced to solipsism and masturbation, no greater danger than the shift from sanctity of life to quality of life and no more forlorn hope than the widening of the meaning of marriage at the same time as a weakening of the bonds of covenant.

"No ties, no tears," say the cool ones, those people whose philosophy when relationships frustrate or fail is always to "move on." But relationships in the traditional view are not a matter of ownership but of belonging. They are not a question of calculation or consumption but of commitment. Freely consenting, mutually binding covenants such as Jewish and Christian marriage do not mean that either member of the couple owns the other, but rather that they belong to each other. *Freedom in this sense is the birthright of those who belong.*

FREEDOM AS TRUTH

The Jewish and Christian way of freedom is a vision of freedom based on truth. According to this view, there is no such thing as bare freedom. Freedom is always tempered freedom, freedom within a framework of truth and virtue. Thus freedom's key question is certainly, "Who governs me?" But while many make sure that the government does not, they are far from resistant to being governed by other unworthy outside influences and are anything but self-governed and truly free.

Freedom requires truth and virtue, for it is only within the framework of what is true and right and good and beautiful that freedom can be found. G. K. Chesterton wrote, "The moment you step into a world of facts, you step into a world of limits. You can free things from alien or accidental laws, but not from the laws of their own nature. You may, if you like, free a tiger from his bars, but do not free him from his stripes. Do not free a camel from his hump: you may be freeing him from being a camel."[22]

Freedom, then, is never simply privacy or freedom from interference or the right to be let alone. Nor is it simply procedural or only a matter of choice, in which the greater the range of choices, the greater the depth of freedom. An endless proliferation of trivial and unworthy choices is not freedom but slavery by another name. Freedom is not choice so much as right choice, good choice and wise choice. When everything is permissible, no one is truly free, so it is ironic but not accidental that millions in "the land of the free" are in recovery groups from one addiction or another.

Freedom is certainly about possibility and choice, but freedom as bare possibility will always end in confusion, just as freedom as infinite change and choice ends only in exhaustion. Freedom requires truth and virtue, and the wisdom of their limits. As the French philosopher Helvétius wrote, "It is not lack of freedom not to fly like an eagle or swim like a whale."[23] Freedom assumes a wise decision about what is believed to be true and good and beautiful—and especially about what a human person is assumed to be.

Freedom will be different for those who believe with Bertrand Russell that humans are a product of chance and an accident in the universe, for those who believe with Peter Singer that humans are no more than animals and for those who believe with Jews and Christians that human dignity is inalienable because it is grounded in the fact that each human person is made in the image of God.

Montesquieu scorned the idea that democratic liberty was when "the people seem pretty much to do what they wish," for that was to "confound the power of the people with the liberty of the people."[24] Rather, he argued, true liberty is "being able to do what one ought to want & and in not being constrained to do what one ought not to want."[25] Similarly, Lord Acton claimed that freedom is "not the power of doing what we like but the right of being able to do what we ought."[26] Freedom is not the permission to do what we like but the power to do what we should.

Winston Churchill often cited the remark of Alexander the Great that the Persians would always be slaves because they did not know the meaning of the word *no*—which is to say that freedom thrives on self-restraint and the power to say no. It rests on strong convictions about what is true and on equally strong constraints against what is false. A culture with no claims on its members—or curbs on their desires—would be a culture with no future. Freedom requires a firm refusal of what is false, what is bad, what is excessive, what is ugly and, above all, what a person is not and should never try to become. When everything is tolerable, nothing will be true; and when nothing is true, no one will be free.

We humans are not free when we tell a lie, do what is wrong, produce what is ugly or treat another human in a way that violates his or her personhood—which means that freedom can never be defended by torture, for a free society that respects human dignity cannot be a torturing society and a torturing society cannot be a free society. Period.

Besides, if rights truly are *inalienable*, as John Locke and the founders claimed emphatically, then no one—absolutely no one, the president and his lawyers included—can waive the right of another without weakening the meaning of rights for all by showing that no right is inalienable. Only one person can waive an inalienable right—the possessor of that right. For anyone else, whether the president, the government or a majority, to waive the right of another is to transgress that person's inalienable rights and commit a despotic act. Once again freedom is a core issue in the question of whether America can torture and still claim to be the land of the free.

In sum, there are things that each of us as free people simply cannot and should not be, and should not do, although we could. The promise that in a free society we can be anything we want to be is a specious modern delusion. The idea that freedom means we can do what we like, so long as we do not hurt anyone else, is a dangerous modern lie.

The sad fact is that without truth and virtue, those who proclaim freedom and set out to do what they like often end up not liking what they have done. *Freedom in this sense is liberty within law, autonomy under authority and obedience to the unenforceable.*

MAN MAKES HIMSELF

The modern secularist view is strongly opposed to this Jewish and Christian view, and it regards the declaration of human autonomy as the heart and soul of the Promethean project of modernity. Through its own secular trinity of reason, freedom and progress, humanity declares and demonstrates that it bows to no authority higher or other than itself. Humanity, in the third Lord Shaftesbury's words, becomes a "second God," responsible for both itself and the world. As this opposing view sees it, contemporary freedom is not a corruption but an advance on traditional freedom. As such, it is the product of three major sources.

The first source is philosophical—the humanist revolution that began in the Renaissance, burst out in the French Revolution, blossomed in the Enlightenment and rose to its climax in the 1960s. It has recently gained a new lease on life from the sunnier side of globalization and the idea that the world is flat or flattening fast, so that we are steadily becoming more united, more free and more prosperous at the same time.

At the heart of this first revolution for autonomy is the Renaissance myth of the human power to choose and to achieve self-creation. It is based on some cardinal claims: that human beings are decisively different from animals, that humans have the freedom to choose and design their own future, and that the overall trajectory of humankind is progress—in short, that Man (humanity) makes himself.

The early, classic statement of the Renaissance view is that of Pico della Mirandola in fifteenth-century Florence, as he imagines God addressing Adam: "You, who are confined by no limits, shall determine for yourself your own nature, in accordance with your own free will. . . . You shall fashion yourself in whatever form you prefer." The result is a staggering new view of Adam and humanity: "To him, it was granted to have what he chooses, to be what he wills."[27]

The same theme rings out from the Renaissance and down the centuries in a variety of expressions:

Leon Batista Alberti: "A man can do all things if he will."[28]

Karl Marx: "Man is free only if he owes his existence to himself."[29]

Friedrich Nietzsche: "If there were gods, who could bear not to be gods? Therefore there are no gods."[30]

Henri Saint-Simon instructed his valet to wake him every morning with the greeting "Remember, monsieur le Comte, that you have great things to do."

Herbert Spencer: "Progress is not an accident, but a necessity. Surely must evil and immorality disappear; surely must men become perfect."[31]

Walt Whitman: "One's-self I sing, a simple separate person."[32]

Julian Huxley: "Today, in twentieth-century man, the evolutionary process is at last becoming conscious of itself."[33]

John F. Kennedy: "Man can be as big as he wants. No problem of human destiny is beyond human beings."[34]

E. O. Wilson: "Genetic evolution is about to become conscious and volitional . . . humanity will be positioned godlike to take control of its own ultimate fate."[35]

Ayn Rand: "Man's destiny is to be a self-made soul."[36]

As many of these assertions show, the first and philosophical source of the secularist view of freedom blends easily into the second: the scientific revolution. Beginning in the seventeenth century, the scientific revolution climaxes theoretically in the therapeutic revolution under Freud and practically in the sexual revolution with its introduction of the Pill. Together, these revolutions appear to give humans a double dividend: the promise of power over both the former limitations of nature and the former restrictions of culture. They therefore provide the practical underpinnings to achieve the dreams of philosophical optimism.

Never mind that, like Renaissance humanism, the modern scientific revolution came out of a Christian matrix and was pioneered almost entirely by devout Christians such as Copernicus, Johannes Kepler, Robert Boyle and Isaac Newton. Science has now outgrown these origins, and in the hands of the Enlightenment humanists, it has become the leading avenue to human self-sufficiency, the principal weapon with which to attack religion and the main tool with which humans can master nature and make themselves—not to mention the principal road to the domination and rape of nature.

Today, this human will to dominate has become self-propelling and profoundly double-edged. Francis Bacon's "knowledge is power" and Max Weber's "instrumental rationality" have given us mastery over nature, taken us to the moon and to undreamed advances in medicine and health, and will soon lead us to the trans-human future. Francis Bacon's "kingdom of Man" has triumphed. He had summoned humans in martial terms to make peace among themselves and then to turn "with united forces against the Nature of Things, to storm and occupy her castles and strongholds, and extend the bounds of human empire."

Several centuries later, what Bacon called "the power and dominion of the human race over the universe," or "the empire of man over things," is complete. Human leaders with this philosophy are his "new princes" who can each go forward to their own "power, glory, amplification, continuance" and become a "god to man."[37] Clearly, such human titans who are gods themselves need have no faith of any kind—except in themselves. There is no one and nothing higher in which to trust than themselves.

The third and most recent source of the secularist view of freedom is the consumerist revolution, which served to spread the benefits of the other two revolutions to ordinary people and to accelerate the spread of free-choice societies. The grand claim that "man makes himself" has descended from Renaissance palaces, scientists' studies and artists' studios to shopping malls, fitness centers and plastic surgery clinics. Free-choice societies are those where freedom is equated with choice and everything is said to be ours for the choosing in the grand cornucopia of options offered by the market:

from your gender to your enhanced body to your partner in whatever configuration to your lifestyle, however flexible and changing, to your religion, however bizarre and ill-considered, and even to your genetic makeup. Life is a project, and self-creation is all. Everything fixed, fated, given or commanded is out. In its place are millions of choices offered to us as freedom, for freedom today is another word for possibility, and the illusion of infinite possibility is conjured out of the magic of endless choice. Call it "doing your own thing," call it "authenticity," or call it "following your inner freedom," but the effect is the same. Gone is everything that comes from the higher and the outside or that is passed down or predetermined by others. What is authentic now is what has been designed, decided, determined by each of us ourselves, acting out of our right to be ourselves and to be let alone. After all, life today is all about each of us. It's all up to us, it's all ours to choose, and it's ours to choose without coercion or interference. As today's secularists admit wryly, they once thought they were atheists, until they woke up and realized they were god.

Nothing symbolizes the magic power of the consumer revolution better than the birth of the credit card, introduced by the Bank of America in California in 1958 as the grand fulfillment of three Ds: debt, desire and democracy. What the credit card has done is transform our modern assessment of value. Value is no longer estimated by the ingenuity and sweat of the labor taken to produce something, but by the degree of satisfaction it promises its purchaser.

The result of the consumer revolution is fourfold: first, a decisive shift from needs to desires and an explosive intensification of desire ("taking the waiting out of wanting," as the early ad for the credit card said); second, a strong reinforcement of vanity and envy, as advertising makes luxuries into necessities and invites each person into a lifelong comparison with others; third, a vast extension of choices, not only in terms of products but also of lifestyles and possible futures; and fourth, of course, an astonishing accumulation of excess, junk and debt.

Do Americans not have the right to consume what they produce as a result of their greater ingenuity and entrepreneurship? Yes, of course, but if all the developed and rapidly developing countries did the same, the earth could no longer afford or sustain the consumption, and the inequities between the rich and the poor would be even starker than they are now.

In short, in the form of the consumer revolution, "Man makes himself" goes far beyond philosophers' studies and scientists' labs to previously undreamed-of offers such as endless pleasure experiences, countless virtual realities, designer babies, sex changes, prolonged lifespans and even the promise of future resurrections from a deep-frozen tomb. Who needs God when you can create yourselves in endless new ways?

Needless to say, the combined effect of these three revolutions—the humanist, the scientific and the consumerist—is to champion the modern, secularist view of freedom as negative freedom, freedom *from* constraint, and to create a sense of human autonomy that is unprecedented in history. Just as science and technology once freed us from the limitations of nature, so consumerism and psychology now free us from the restrictions of culture. Old inhibitions have been swamped by new permissions. We are now beckoned to life on a new plateau of liberty, where freedom is freedom from interference, the right to be let alone, the space to do our own thing and the license to make and remake ourselves as often as we desire and need to.

The net effect is decisive for American life and American society. The social/sexual revolution of the last generation has been the final blow that has shattered the bounds of three thousand years of Jewish and then Christian moral understanding, and ushered in what is a perfect storm of relativism.

First, and over the longest time, we have seen the triumph of philosophical relativism ("truth is dead," "knowledge is power," "everything is possible"). To that, and largely since World War II, has been added consumer relativism ("there is no ruling way of life, only fashions," "no rules, only options," "everyone can be anyone"). And now, in the last generation, we have seen the arrival of a relational relativism ("do no harm," "make no judgments," "do anything with anyone in any way, so long as you both consent").

In sum, with the triumph of this triple relativism, negative freedom has driven positive freedom from the field in much of American life. For most Americans and for all practical purposes, God is dead, and nothing—no ethics, no identity, no relationship, no revaluation of all values—is now impossible.

In sum, modern secularist freedom is the dream of life as endless private possibility and continuous experimenting. Lured by this vision, Americans appear closer than ever to the place where they need submit to no power higher than themselves, and the power to create themselves is in their own hands.

NOT SO FAST

At first sight, this description seems enough by itself to show which side holds the advantage. Clearly there can be no sitting on the fence. The two different views lead in entirely opposite directions. America cannot have it both ways. And clearly the trump cards appear to be in the hands of the forces of the secular and liberal views of freedom. Their ideas have a powerful popular appeal, and they are reinforced by the hi-tech trends of modern culture. Yet the secular and humanist view of freedom faces a mounting series of criticisms that could amount to a serious backlash.

First, fellow secularists have raked the foundations of this secular humanism with withering fire. The philosopher John Gray, for example, who is a nonhumanist secularist, has been merciless in exposing the religious assumptions of secular humanism. This sort of humanism, he argues, rests on borrowed Jewish and Christian assumptions about human dignity and freedom (coming from the much-derided book of Genesis), so humanism cannot both reject the earlier faiths and at the same time pretend it rests on premises that are scientific and rational. "Humanism," Gray concludes bluntly, "is a secular religion thrown together from the decaying scraps of Christian myth."[38]

Most Jews and Christians do not regard their faiths as myth in that sense, but they would share Gray's objection. One of the giant question marks over secular humanism is whether its foundations will prove solid, or whether the wax on its borrowed wings will melt and plunge it, Icarus-like, back to earth.

Take, for example, the powerful explosion of concerns for human solidarity over the last generation—and for freedom, justice and human rights, for international compassion, for the health of the earth and for the rights of indigenous peoples. All in all, it is stunning, one of the greatest movements of humanitarian concern in history—and to an unprecedented extent much of it is secularly inspired. But if political and economic circumstances darken, will such idealism be sustained on the basis of secular humanism? The prospect is unlikely, yet Western humanists still insist that they can succeed where their communist partners failed so criminally and that they will be the only successful civilization in history built on decisively secularist foundations. The stakes on their wager are high.

Second, secular humanism confronts the brutal dismissal of the anti-humanists, who in the form of such postmodern radicals as Michel Foucault trace their roots to Nietzsche and scorn the sunny humanist illusions inflated by the Enlightenment. Life is more than ordinary life; it includes death and violence that must be celebrated too. And our very ideals are not what they appear to be. Secular humanism not only has no base, it ignores the "genealogy of morals" that shows how the very pity that relieves suffering is really a disguised form of resentment driven by the "will to power." So widely held has this postmodern view become that philosopher Charles

Taylor describes the culture war not as a war between two extremes but as a "three cornered" battle between traditionalists, secular humanists and anti-humanists.[39]

Third, the secular humanist view is charged with playing dangerously to the most sacred of all American sacred cows: the autonomous self. In the infamous words of Howard Roark, Ayn Rand's grand libertarian in *The Fountainhead*, "I came here today to say that I do not recognize anyone's right to one minute of my life . . . that I am a man who does not exist for others."[40] To be sure, the millions who post their "Daily Me" on Facebook are less brazen, but such higher selfishness has a consistent logic within the worldview of secularism. And the endless self-preoccupation is only an exaggeration of an old American tendency made more common in an age in which Margaret Thatcher famously told readers of a women's magazine in 1987, "You know, there is no such thing as society."[41]

As historian Wilfred McClay points out, American views of the self and society, the individual and the community, have never been well balanced. "Perhaps nowhere else in history have 'self' and 'society' been more likely to be conceived in diametrical opposition to one another."[42] After all, as Tocqueville warned earlier, "not only does democracy make every man forget his ancestors, but it hides his descendants and separates his contemporaries from him; it throws him back forever on himself alone and threatens in the end to confine him entirely with the solitude of his own heart."[43]

Fourth, critics point out how the ironies and unintended consequences of the secularist revolution are now clearer than ever. Consider, for example, the new challenges brought to us by the technological revolution. Life at warp speed (say, in business, Wall Street or war at the speed of light) is so fast that it can be handled only by an increasing reliance on automation, which undercuts time for human deliberation and decision, which undercuts the possibility of human freedom and responsibility. Where now is the Enlightenment dream of a world led only by human reason? The faster we go, the less free, the less reflective and the less responsible we are.

Or again, consider the ironies of the sexual revolution. Those who set out to liberate sex from the cramping constraints of morality and tradition have emptied it of meaning and made it freer, less meaningful, and more chaotic and dangerous at the same time. The newly liberated sex is dangerous not just in the obvious sense of the risks of pregnancy and disease, but in the subtler irony of where unrestrained sex has led America socially. In America, every man is now every woman's potential assailant, and every woman is now every man's potential accuser. Far from *Playboy*'s promised return to an Eden of easy Polynesian delights, Americans find themselves in a wilderness of broken hearts, lonely lives and an uneasy state of suspicion between the sexes.

Or yet again, consider what happens when the therapeutic revolution replaces old categories such as the distinction between *allowed* and *forbidden* with the new distinction between *possible* and *impossible*. "There is no more guilt!" cry the cheerleaders for the couch-freed libertines. No one need suffer hang-ups from repression and prohibitions any longer. There are none. But before our bright, young cheerleaders have ended their dance and put away their pompoms, a new contagion has broken out behind them. In a world of too many possibilities, advanced modern hang-ups are all about feelings of inadequacy and anxiety. Guilt has been repressed, but neuroses and restlessness remain.

Fifth, consider how the consumer revolution never really delivers on its promise of satisfaction and does not intend to. In many ways, consumerism makes us less free, not more. It seduces and betrays us with its promise to satisfy not only our needs but also our desires and even our wishes. But behind the thousand irresistible offers is the fine print. Far from really wanting to satisfy our desires, let alone our needs, the true goal of consumerism is for us to shop and buy, and then to stoke dissatisfaction and seduce us with ever-newer products to satisfy ever-newly awakened desires. The sovereign consumer quickly becomes the seduced consumer. The king ends up as dupe. Sixth, the very notion that "Man makes himself" is under sharp scrutiny after the last two centuries' evidence of the horrendous agendas that this modernist idea has served. The barbarous cruelty of Hitler's doctors and the malevolence of his "final solution" are only the darkest in the long list of horrors that includes eugenics, forced migrations, ethnic cleansing and abortions by the tens of millions.

"Man makes himself" is another way of saying that Man (humankind) made in the image of Man easily becomes the product of Man; and what Man has the license to make, Man also has the license to manipulate, to destroy—and in a word, to unmake. In short, the brave new secularist claim that Man makes himself becomes hubris in a brazen and destructive form. When Man presumes it is its own origin and its own self-sufficiency, the outcome is not only staggering human triumphs, but the devaluing of human dignity, the disarmament of moral conscience, the degradation of the earth and what has been called "the drying of souls."[44]

What follies will this hubris yet produce? For men, women and societies wrapped up only in themselves will always end as fools. But that is only the beginning. When to the core Prometheanism of the modern project is added the privatization bred by consumerism, the narcissism of the culture of authenticity, the essential selfishness of libertarianism and the total relativism of modern anything-goes relationships, the triumph of negative freedom is complete and given a devilish twist. Purely private freedom, turning in on itself and closing itself off from the claims of wider public good, becomes demonic. Jean Paul Sartre's "hell is other people" descends to John Milton's Satanic cry, "Myself am Hell."

What fresh victims will be the next to be thrown on the pyramids of sacrifice that honor the great gods of Pride, Power, Progress and Personal Freedom? Who will follow the Jews, the gypsies, the handicapped and the aborted unborn who have died by the millions already? If allowed Jefferson's first right, the primordial dignity of life itself, America's aborted unborn since Roe v. Wade would now stand before the world tall and strong as more than fifty million citizens and populate a country the size of Britain. Who will be next? Mercifully, perhaps, we cannot see too far into the future. But Americans, with their dark history of eugenics before the Nazis, dare not close their eyes. For those with ears to hear, such warnings should sound the alarm now.

Seventh, postmodern ideas have shifted America from faith-directed beliefs to fiction-directed beliefs and have cut the heart out of progressive views of human enlightenment and progress. Contrary to what Jefferson said, no truths are self-evident now. At best, the deep things of life are said to be indeterminate and undecidable. At worst, nothing is what it appears to be. Everything is ultimately an expression of the will to power, so that in area after area victory goes to the strong, and the weak go to the wall. As one student declared at a Harvard commencement, "The freedom of our day is the freedom to devote ourselves to any values we please, on the mere condition that we do not believe them to be true."[45]

The force of these combined objections is powerful. Yet the fact is that the modern, secularist ideal of freedom is now rampaging through America, even in religious circles, and it will never be stopped by theory alone. For one thing, the supporting power of modern technologies and lifestyles is too strong. For another, there is a perverse alliance between secular-liberal accounts of freedom and economic-conservative (or neoliberal) accounts of freedom, both of which have a deficient understanding of the place of ethics, community and solidarity. Combined, their views of freedom are doing profound damage to America, but they cannot be criticized in theory alone.

The coming wasteland of glittering emptiness, loneliness and brokenness has to be countered by an alternative vision that is not only stated but lived out persuasively as a lifestyle and a robust counter-

culture. Yet in the case of the American culture wars, the alternative
vision is all too often handicapped by incoherence in thought and
inconsistencies in life. For all their troubled consciences, too many
Americans on both sides of the culture wars are already de facto supporters of modern, secularist freedom. At the level of lifestyle, most
Americans are practicing secularists now, just as most conservatives
are more liberal than they realize.

SO LONG AGO,
YET SO UP-TO-DATE

The prevailing strength of the secularist-liberal view of freedom is
clear, but where will it lead? Suffice it to say that to any reader of
history, and in particular any student of the brilliant insights of
Montesquieu and Tocqueville, it is astonishing how close the two
Frenchmen were to seeing where the United States has come today in
terms of a fateful dualism that American life has bred.

On the one hand, Tocqueville foresaw democracy producing a
trend toward egalitarian *individualism*. This term is commonly used
today, but it was coined by the young Frenchman to describe his
equivalent of Nietzsche's "last men"—those mediocre souls who were
devoted only to their own health and happiness. Nothing could be
further from the robust, self-reliant American citizens that Tocqueville admired: citizens who had learned to think for themselves and
to rely on themselves without the support of outside help or the government.

I see an innumerable multitude of me, alike and equal, who
turn about without repose in order to procure for themselves
petty and vulgar pleasures with which to fill their souls.
Each of them, withdrawn apart, is a virtual stranger, unaware of the fate of the others: his children and his particular
friends form for him the entirety of the human race; as for
his fellow citizens, he is beside them but he sees them not; he

touches them and senses them not; he exists only in himself and for himself alone, and, if he still has a family, one could say at least that he no longer has a fatherland.[46]

On the other hand, Tocqueville saw a parallel trend to what Montesquieu had called the "administrative state" and that he called the "soft despotism" and "tutelary power" of government. This is George Orwell's Big Brother and Margaret Thatcher's Nanny State in a benign democratic form, through which "the sovereign extends its arms about the society as a whole." If such soft despotism brings chains, they are golden chains and self-chosen. After all, citizens of a free society who eschew tyranny but choose a tutelary state "console themselves with the thought that they have chosen the tutors themselves."[47] In short, Americans today all seem bent on turning themselves into Uncle Sam's pensioners and are happy to pay any price to do so.

> Over these is elevated an immense tutelary power, which takes sole charge of assuring their enjoyment and watching over their fate. It is absolute, attentive to detail, regular, provident, and gentle. . . . It does not break wills; it softens them, bends them, and directs them; rarely does it force one to act, but it constantly opposes itself to one's acting on one's own; it does not destroy, it prevents things from being born; it does not tyrannize, it gets in the way; it curtails, it enervates, it extinguishes, it stupefies, and finally it reduces each nation to nothing more than a herd of timid and industrious animals, of which the government is the shepherd.[48]

BEWARE THE HORSESHOE SYNDROME

Such eighteenth-century prescience is astonishing as well as haunting, and its challenge for the present freedom war is plain. For, like a horseshoe, the two trends come closest and touch at the extremes. The triumph of the modern, secularist view takes the negative aspect of freedom to excess, undermines the ordered liberty necessary for a republic and breeds a democracy of appetites that hungers for an all-catering state. Thus Tocqueville's twin tendencies appear contradictory, but they actually feed off each other. Both the rampant individualism of American private life and the all-devouring American sense of entitlement encourage the state to expand in the name of caring for its citizens. The sovereign individual and the sovereign state are closer than people realize.

In short, such a lopsided view of freedom, especially when reinforced by the power of the credit card, beckons like a glittering paradise for consumers. But it also undermines the founders' view of sustainable freedom. It would mean the end of the self-restraint that is the essence of freedom. It would spell the end of Tocqueville's habits of the heart and the end of the golden triangle of freedom that underlies the founders' way to sustain freedom.

Needless to say, in the end it will mean the end of American freedom itself. And with a savage flip of the coin, freedom's glittering indulgence of unrestrained wishes, fantasies and instincts will be recognized for what it is—the other side of the unrestrained impulses that are addiction, slavery and mediocrity by another name.

To be sure, critics will say that we have heard such jeremiads before, whether voices from the past such as Tocqueville's or voices from around the world such as America's critics. It is true that no merely theoretical debate will settle the argument, for while any thoughts can be thought, not all thoughts can be lived. The contest will be settled in the courts of experience, history and death.

If the two origins, the two worldviews and the two ways of life behind the two views of freedom are so different, what of their outcomes? By their fruit we will know them, so we need to follow their assumptions all the way out to their conclusions. The present choice is one thing; tomorrow's consequences are another. In Jewish history, there is an account of a time when there was no authority in Israel, and "everyone did as they saw fit" (Judges 21:25). Similarly in the history of Greece, Xenophon told of a moment when Athenian democracy became so corrupt that the people cried out that it was monstrous to stop them doing whatever they pleased. Tradition had so little authority, law so little restraint and virtue so little appeal that the rights of the minority and the responsibilities of the majority were all disregarded equally.

Could American freedom degenerate and slide toward that condition? Could either soft nihilism or soft despotism morph into a harder version? Could there ever be an American Augustus, who would so establish his own and the state's power that a return to republican freedom would be impossible? Doubtless there will be voices lamenting the menace of the Caesars and their smooth massaging of the public through "bread and circuses." But Americans have to go back only to Tocqueville's great mentor, Montesquieu. He analyzed Rome's sad shift from republic to empire, and in an uncanny anticipation of Napoleon warned that no authority is more absolute than that of a leader who succeeds a republic, "for he finds himself in possession of all the power of a People incapable of putting limits on itself."[49] Perpetually restless and dissatisfied people are dream clients for a strong man or woman and mere putty in his or her hands.

But we need not stray into guessing about the future. In America there is already a tension between individual freedom and stable, caring community. It would be fateful if the two were to become alternatives rather than allies. On one side, many liberals and libertarians, who view freedom as negative freedom (freedom from interference), attack all impediments to individual freedom—usually in the name of the widening revolution of rights. They are reinforced by contemporary notions of authenticity, now taken to mean that any moral standard outside oneself is an unwarranted barrier against being true to oneself. Many therefore wish to make the right to be left alone not only the beginning but the goal and sum of freedom. Similarly, many survivalists cry, "Don't tread on me," and join supporters of the National Rifle Association in replacing religious liberty and free speech by making the right to bear arms the "first liberty."

What would happen if the secularist and progressive view of freedom had its way, and these trends went to the end of the line? Beyond question, the tilt is presently in that direction, for even those who do not understand or agree with the philosophy and the causes behind it are caught up in the worlds of science, technology and consumerism that make it self-evident for now.

Futurism is a quack science, and the only certainty is the uncertainty of the "improbable consequential" of Nassim Taleb's "black swan events." So I make no predictions. But let me simply point out how the logic of contemporary American freedom, fueled by the modern, secularist philosophy, the therapeutic revolution, a free-market mentality and the postmodern mistrust of authority—and increasingly uninhibited by traditional constraints—is already showing signs of the excesses that will only grow worse. Americans decry the nihilism of radical Islam, but advanced modern American freedom has itself become nihilistic. It is a soft though decadent nihilism that devours tradition, destroys social cohesion, cheapens cultural standards, hollows moral convictions and in the years to come will produce its own dark harvest of social consequences.

One foreseeable crisis is the shock created by the collision of three trends: the radical relativism of the anything-goes relationships that will create a harvest of singles, loners and quietly desperate people; the deepening economic crisis; and the absolute inability of the guardian state to take over the emotional roles and social functions of the collapsed family. Only then, if too late, will it be clear which of the two traditions was the more realistic and sustainable.

In sum, America has now strayed further from the practical realism of the founders than many realize, and it is now nearer to

Chesterton's "ultimate test" and Bryce's "completest revolution." Before long, the curtain will rise on the denouement. So again Americans must never forget: all who aspire to be like Rome in their beginnings must avoid being like Rome at their ending. Rome and its republic fell, and so too will the American republic—unless . . .

6

An Empire Worthy
of Free People

"To be born English is to have won first prize in the lottery of life." That proud claim, attributed alternately to Cecil Rhodes and Rudyard Kipling, has long since lost the luster it had in 1900 when a third of the world lived under the Union Jack and the sun, quite literally, never set on the British Empire. More recently, life's grand prize has gone to those who are born American.

And tomorrow? The very source of the quotation should give Americans pause. Kipling's own life was enough to span the fleeting moment from the zenith of the British Empire to its decline, and he was keenly aware of the long, slow ebb of empire. The recurring line in his poem "Recessional" is "Lest we forget—lest we forget!" and at its heart is a stern reminder worthy of the realism of the classical age:

Lo, all our pomp of yesterday
Is one with Nineveh and Tyre![1]

Kipling published his poem "White Man's Burden" in 1899 at a critical moment in the Philippine-American War, which itself was a critical moment in the rise of American imperialism. The poem is often taken as a slogan for imperialism, but it was heavy with irony—a warning to Americans who were taking over the imperial mission from the English and would one day weary of the burden in their turn.

The American founders would have been no strangers to such ironies and to such a sense of time and decay. Yet they would surely be disappointed at the thoughtlessness with which their protections have been ignored, their provisions set aside and their limits broken through—for the U.S. Constitution and the golden triangle of freedom were together meant to be the civic equivalent of *ne plus ultra* (no further beyond), which was the traditional Spanish understanding of Gibraltar and the Pillars of Hercules.

The twenty-first century adds a fresh twist to the story that turns history's winning lottery into a poisoned prize. History in the global era no longer represents a single, linear progression from one Western superpower to another, as it has over the last five hundred years. If that were so, the infamous neoconservative thinking of the memos from the Project for the New American Century would be correct. The United States, like some prodigious bull moose, would only have to look around the West and watch for the next young buck that threatens to rival its dominance.

Instead, the movement of history in the global era is more like an exploding constellation of competitors in the grand global game of different ways to be modern. Suddenly, as power diffuses all around the world, the great beast is not the only bull in the herd, and the moose are not the only herd in the forest.

Thus, contrary to Francis Fukuyama, Americans have not reached "the end of history." Contrary to the National Security Council, there is no "single sustained model of success" in modernity. Contrary to advocates of realpolitik, America's "unipolar moment" in a world of "multiple modernities" may be brief. And contrary to twentieth-century liberals, there is no "rational consensus" to which all reasonable people will subscribe. Globalization is not Westernization, and Westernization is not Americanization. Neither freedom nor democracy nor free markets will prevail universally; and contrary to the second President Bush and his neoconservative henchmen, there will be no lasting triumph for freedom, justice or peace, and the earth will not be rid of tyranny and evil.

All such utopianism runs aground on the reality of human nature. The world is still flawed, we still live on a blighted star, humanity is still constructed with crooked timber, and the world is now closer to Nietzsche's prediction of "war of spirits" than to Kant's vision of a "world republic" and "perpetual peace." The future of the global era is still likely to be one of deepening diversity and endless kinds of conflict, often bordering on anarchy, and with failed and failing states sometimes as perversely influential as world powers.

To believe otherwise is to be deluded by hubris, as many Americans were in the twelve sunny years between the fall of the wall in 1989 and the fall of the towers in 2001. What America saw in the collapse of the Soviet Union was the triumph of the West. What much of the rest of the world saw was the triumph of one Western ideology over another Western ideology and the global opening of the door to a post-American and post-Western era in which other ways to be modern are having their own say. In the global era, with new technologies of communication and old, asymmetric ways of waging war, the once-powerless are no longer so and the once all-powerful are less powerful than they thought.

In short, the global era confronts Americans with a thousand questions directed at the heart of what the great American republic stands for in the wider world. Singly and together, they underscore the importance of the second level at which American freedom has to be tested: the international arena. Are Americans abroad demonstrating and sustaining freedom in a manner worthy of a free republic or have the founders' designs been cast aside in pursuit of superpower goals and responsibilities?

WHAT PRICE EMPIRE?

Can the United States be a superpower that is worthy of free people? Is it right for a free people to maintain what Montesquieu called "unceasing superiority" over other people, as the National Security Council called for. Or was the Frenchman correct that "a thing like this has become morally impossible"?[2] Is there any point to empty American boasts of parallels with Rome when the United States cannot and should not be like Rome? And is it even wise to seek perpetual superpower dominance at a time when, as Montesquieu warned and the war in Afghanistan underlines, "victory impoverishes not only the vanquished but the victor as well," and when "today's victories confer none but sterile laurels"?[3]

There are four tests in the arena of international standing. America must prove its mettle in each as a superpower worthy of free people or fail as another passing form of empire by whatever name. The first test is to see whether American leaders can articulate America's role as the world's supreme power concerned with universal liberty in a global age aware of the different ways of being modern. America's economic and military dominance is not in question, at least not yet. What is at issue is America's accompanying political wisdom that is triggering strong responses to the exercise of its dominant power. Burke warned the British at a similar stage of dominance:

> Among precautions against ambition, it may not be amiss to take precautions against our own. I must fairly say, I dread our own power and our own ambition; I dread our being too much dreaded. . . . We may say that we shall not abuse this astonishing and hitherto unheard of power. But every other nation will think we shall abuse it. It is impossible but that, sooner or later, this state of things must produce a combination against us which may end in our ruin.[4]

Americans can claim that their military, economic and cultural power still stands at an unprecedented and unrivalled level. But only just. Presidential speeches notwithstanding, America's relationship to freedom and global diversity has grown far less clear in the last decade. Attempts to assert America's sole superpower strength unilaterally have caused disquiet and anger around the world and called into question what America means by freedom and more simply, what America means to the world. To much of the world today, the United States is increasingly unwanted or irrelevant.

Strikingly, America once spoke for the world, over against European colonialism; but today Europe often speaks for the world, over against American imperialism. Or the more modest America was about her uniqueness, the more appealing America was; whereas the more America presses her universality, the less universal is her appeal. Once an extraordinary nation, the United States has behaved like an all too ordinary empire.

It will not do to equate America and freedom and then to assume that any and all American policies are automatically justified in the name of freedom.

It will not do for Americans to rehearse their good intentions, for in the age of side effects, unintended consequences and unknown aftermaths, the best intentions may produce the worst of results and pave the road to another manmade hell.

It will not do for Americans to keep reciting their traditional anti-imperialism, for empires are the closest historical parallel to America's present dominance.

It will not do for Americans to resort to euphemisms and speak of themselves as a "reluctant empire," an "undeclared empire," a "de facto empire," an "empire by any other name," "an empire that dare not name its name" or "an empire in denial."[5] An empire by any name at all is still an empire.

It will not do for Americans to compare apples with oranges and make false comparisons with other kinds of empire. Americans often say with pride or in self-justification—most recently in Afghanistan and Iraq—that they are not conquerors or occupiers, as if all empires were conquered on the pattern of Alexander the Great and Julius Caesar.

To be sure, America's dominance is not an empire of the roads and swords, based on military force and the conquest of a large landmass. Nor is it like the Portuguese and Spanish dominance, an empire of the winds and waves, built on maritime force and the ability to go around the world. Nor again, though here the comparison is closer, is American dominance quite like the Dutch and British empires, empires of stocks and bonds, based on mercantile power and held together only loosely by force. Clive of India described British imperialism as a matter of trade, not territory.

Empires have never been all of one kind. Their only common element is the spread of their dominance. A famous nineteenth-century English cartoon showed William Pitt the Younger and Napoleon Bonaparte slicing up an enormous global pudding with their swords—the Frenchman tucking into the continents and the Englishman devouring the seas. The empire of the elephant and the empire of the whale were both voracious, but their appetites were different.

The same is true of the United States today. The claim to the right to outer space may be as strategically important to America today as the right to the land, the right to the sea and the right to the air were each in their turn, but the pretensions of the imperial reach are the same in each case.

In 1916, President Wilson drafted the speech in which he declared, "It shall not lie with the American people to dictate to another what their government shall be." His Secretary of State Robert Lansing wrote in the margin: "Haiti, S Domingo, Nicaragua, Panama."[6] That list could be greatly extended today. The slave's voice in the victor's ear and the truth teller's note in the president's margin are more needed than ever to remind Americans of their imperial reach and its consequences in the eyes of others.

What, then, is the character of American "empire" in the global era?

At the time of England's emerging new understanding of empire in the sixteenth century, Sir Walter Raleigh wrote candidly about what lay at its core: "Whosoever commands the sea, commands the trade; whosoever commands the trade of the world, commands the riches of the world and consequently the world itself."[7] We need a similar clarity and candor about America's self-understanding today, for there are three unavoidable facts that bar an American slide into an imperial posture like that of the empires of the past.

First is the flinty precedent and prudence of the American founders, with their clear teaching about the need for a "decent respect" for the opinions of the world, the dangers of excessive foreign "influences" and of "entanglement" in the affairs of other nations, and their warning that in riding out to "slay monsters," the United States could become a monster in its turn.

Second is the clear and courageous tradition of American anti-imperialism, from the struggle for independence from the British Empire in 1776 to the open opposition to the European empires under Franklin Roosevelt and Dwight Eisenhower. That history, and the effect of America's careful buildup of international institutions to make arbitrary force less thinkable, meant that the Iraq War was a bitter disappointment to many of America's admirers. It mocked the very gift that had been America's shining contribution to the modern world.

Third is the awkward fact that America's universalizing mission clashes head-on with an essential feature of empires in history. Long-lasting empires, from Rome to Turkey to Austria to Great Britain, have been multicultural projects abroad, however homogeneous at home. They used their dominant power to unite diverse cultures into a grand whole by tolerating their differences. It would be ironic indeed if the United States, which at home is one of the most multicultural great powers in history, were to be rejected vehemently because it forgot its own multicultural realities when it went overseas and attempted to impose its American Way of freedom and free markets on everyone, everywhere, in the same way.

LESSONS OF EMPIRE

A second test is for America to show that it has learned the lessons of imperialism and will follow a quite different course. Empires throughout history have shown many of the same dynamics and challenges as nations, ending always in decline. The first stage of empire is the imperial parallel to winning freedom: the *expansion* of empire. If power is the capacity to exert will despite resistance, then the growth of empire is the expansion of power over wide territories, creating what the Roman historian Tacitus called "an immense body of empire." For military empires, such expansion was through conquest. For mercantile empires, it was through competition.

Imperial expansion has always been fired by the dynamism of an unbounded faith and the spirit of its vision—"something that you can set up, and bow down before," as Joseph Conrad describes it in *Heart of Darkness*.[8] The Romans boasted that Terminus, the god of boundaries, refused to be present at Rome's birth. Similarly, Charles V of Spain defied the traditional *Ne Plus Ultra* of the Rock of Gibraltar and sent his ships out to the New World with their sails emblazoned with the words *Plus ultra* (Further beyond). In line with such expansiveness, the ambitious slogan of the U.S. Air Force was "Global Power, Global Reach."

The second stage of empire is the imperial parallel to ordering freedom: *inclusion*. Talleyrand described empire as "the art of putting men in their place," and Churchill called this stage an empire's ability to "digest" what it had won.[9] Various strategies have been employed to achieve this inclusion. The Greeks set up "colonies" to be missionary outposts of Hellenism, Rome offered citizenship to its subjugated peoples, and Britain's celebrated policy of "indirect rule" was described as the best of British bluff, or "a triumph of minimalism."[10] (The British Empire in India ruled over 350 million Indians through the Indian Civil Service, which was led by fewer than a thousand Europeans.)

The third stage of empire is the imperial parallel to sustaining freedom, or more accurately, of its failure: *overextension through empire-creep*. Empires inevitably make wider and wider commitments until they are overwhelmed by the impossibility of sustaining them all. In the words of Heraclides of Byzantium to Scipio Africanus cited earlier, "It was easier to gain it [empire] part by part than to hold the whole."[11] Or as Sir Thomas More observed about the costs of empire in *Utopia:* "Eventually they won, only to find that the kingdom in question was quite as much trouble to keep as it had been to acquire."[12]

However easy it is to gain an empire, no empire can hold it all together forever, and the logic is there for Americans to observe. Too large to rule, too diverse to unite, too expensive to afford and too far-flung to defend, empire after empire suffered from the accumulated overreach of its easy, earlier expansions.

Seneca described Alexander the Great as "swollen beyond the limits of human arrogance." Thomas More advised the king of France to "forget about Italy and stay at home."[13] Montaigne and Pascal reminded us that all kings and presidents sit not only on their thrones but also on their backsides.[14] In sum, all human endeavors that stretch beyond their human reach collapse in the end.

So too will America's vaunted dominance—especially if, as Ferguson comments, the American empire is a "short-winded empire" of "Ivy League nation builders" that is "without settlers," "without administrators" and without true native knowledge of the places it seeks to control. In the blunt words of one CIA case officer, who admitted that most case officers live in the suburbs of Virginia, "operations that include diarrhea as a way of life don't happen."[15]

Americans commonly brag that they spend as much on their defense and armed forces as the next twenty-five nations combined, but the boast has suddenly become a burden. America's overstretched military in Afghanistan and Iraq was a microcosm of the way the United States is massively overextended in today's world. The real loser is the American citizen deprived of the benefits of a prosperity that should have created a better and more just society at home. Americans find themselves at the point where they are always in harm's way, yet show no signs of knowing how to come home. Besides, when Americans brag that everything from business to politics to war is conducted "at the speed of light," how can they not expect their time of dominance to end rapidly too?

Will America follow the precedent of its founders and use history to defy history, and so avoid the normal course of empire? Here also there are three awkward facts that confront America as a warning.

First, Americans have characteristically short memories and even shorter political cycles, so they act in sharp contrast to their founders and display an ignorance of history and the world that is a fatal handicap to lasting dominance. If Europeans remember too much, Americans forget too much. Anti-Americanism certainly represents a distorted view of America, but the American media—from television to films to advertisements to video games—represent an equally deformed view of history and the world.

Second, Americans do not have the willingness to assume the long-term costs of dominance, whether militarily, economically or in the lives and blood of young men and women.

Third, Americans thrive on a doctrinaire optimism, which for all its admirable qualities is a serious weakness when it comes to living wisely within realistic limits in a fallen world.

Such obstacles stand in the way of sustained world leadership, not to speak of lasting world dominance. Indeed, Ferguson estimates that America's "attention deficit" far outweighs the menace of her economic deficit and manpower deficit, and reduces America to being "a sedentary colossus" or "a kind of strategic couch potato."[16]

With such deficiencies, the United States faces three broad options: to overcome these challenges and open up the possibility of enduring influence, to face them squarely and renounce her universalizing mission accordingly, or simply to drift blindly toward a disastrous schizophrenia as America remains economically and militarily engaged all around the world but grows more and more isolated in her domestic thinking and culture.

TO SEE OURSELVES AS OTHERS SEE US

A third test is for America to show that it can avoid the perils of all dominant powers in its relationship to the rest of the world and in particular the blindness that the Greeks called *hubris*. Far more than simply pride, hubris to the Greeks was a crime worse than patricide and incest. It was an overweening arrogance and presumption that created an illusion of invulnerability, which led to the tragic downfall of individuals and nations.

The United States claims to have ubiquity, omnivoyance and omnipresence. Such boasts about the godlike capacities of a global superpower are understandable. But the illusions and the vulnerabilities are as evident too. The result is America Agonistes, prodigious in its power, but in the eyes of many around the world, prodigal in its blindness, folly and destructiveness.

Above all, there is the temptation of the ancient conceit that a great nation's supremacy derives directly from its virtues and its prowess, rather than from providence or any accidents of history—though with a very different logic, the same nation's failures are always said to derive from events beyond anyone's control.

Americans might ponder two quotations. One is the much-cited, self-congratulatory saying attributed to Tocqueville (but whose source no one has so far been able to show me): "America is great because America is good." The other is the very real saying of Samuel Johnson, attacking the similar self-congratulatory "greatness" of the English: "We continue every day to show by new proofs, that no people can be great who have ceased to be virtuous."[17]

From this first conceit grows a further illusion that what is good for a superpower is automatically good for the rest of the world. "What is good for the French is good for everybody," Napoleon said.[18] "We are the first race in the world," the nineteenth-century British said, "and the more of the world we inhabit, the better it is for the human race."[19]

From such conceits grows the fatal hubris-inspired illusion that an empire can afford to treat human beings elsewhere differently than its own citizens. American leaders who defend their record on torture and human rights should ponder the words of Supreme Court Justice Robert Jackson. As chief American counsel at the Nuremberg trial of the Nazi leaders, he adamantly rejected all double standards: "If certain acts of violations of treaties are crimes, they are crimes whether the United States does them or whether Germany does them, and we are not prepared to lay down a rule of criminal conduct against others which we would not be willing to have invoked against us."[20]

If the rule of law is fundamental to America, it must be fundamental for America across the world, and it is hypocritical for America to boast of the rule of law while insisting that it can be above the law when it wants to be. Nothing is more dangerous than a combination of arrogance, lack of self-awareness and double standards. From such blindness grows in turn the final illusion of empire: that its success will somehow be enduring even though no empire has endured before. Thus superpowers on which the sun truly never sets geographically become superpowers that live as if the sun will never set on them historically.

Hubris always breeds insensitivities and particularly the insensitivity that makes empires oblivious to the costs of their dominance to others. Here, too, America must consider three facts.

First, there is a serious gap between America's view of itself and the world's view of America. The United States sees itself as a universal model for the world and as having a universal mission to the world. But to put the point charitably, its generous vision is finding a chilly reception in many parts of the world today.

Second, there is an equally serious gap between America's view of its mission and its assumption of what it will take to achieve it. The goal of bringing freedom, democracy and free markets to the world is one thing, but the idea that it can somehow fulfill this mission without shouldering the normal costs, casualties and oppositions of the burdens of empire is quite another.

Third, there is a fateful gap between America's general other-directedness domestically and her common obliviousness internationally. With notable exceptions, America at home is suffering from an overdose of what David Riesman called "other-directedness"— too much peer influence, too many polls and too much pandering. It could do with an overall return to the "inner-directedness" of earlier Western leaders such as Winston Churchill and Harry Truman. "I hear it said," the prime minister declared in a speech in the House of Commons on September 30, 1941, "that leaders should keep their ears to the ground. All I can say is that the British nation will find it very hard to look up to the leaders who are detected in that somewhat ungainly posture." Truman said, "I wonder how far Moses would have gone if he had taken a poll in Egypt."[21]

Yet, paradoxically, the same America that is other-directed domestically often appears oblivious to others internationally. The United States under George W. Bush was known for its tin ear at the very moment when anti-Americanism was reaching a new crescendo, like a one-fingered wave rolling around the vast stadium that is world opinion in the global era. There are many reasons for American ignorance of the world—indifference to history, lack of travel, the entertainment bias of American television, the corporate refusal to pay for serious international news and so on. But together they add up to the fact that most Americans are dangerously unaware of what is going on in most parts of the world. If Washington is right to operate on the maxim that "the perception is the reality," then Americans must understand the reality that is seen around the world, even if the perception is distorted and false.

Australian ethicist Peter Singer has lamentable views of human dignity, but his concern for global ethics is admirable and his sober conclusion on American leadership would be widely supported around the world: "It has to be said, in cool but plain language, that in recent years the international effort to build a global community has been hampered by the repeated failure of the United States to play its part. . . . If it does not, it risks falling into a situation in which it is universally seen by everyone except its own self-satisfied citizens as the world's 'rogue superpower.'"[22]

Are such criticisms fair, and do they matter? Rome was not built in a day nor governed by opinion polls. Besides, the charges are often contradictory, such as the jibe that Americans are both Puritans and pornographers, morally uptight as well as self-indulgent. Obvious replies can be made to many of the charges. But what matters is that America's view of itself is unrecognizable to much of the world, and the gap is now so wide that no amount of "public diplomacy" and "rebranding" can redeem such vast imperial vanity or put Humpty Dumpty together again. "Brand America" is in trouble, but as much of the world sees it, America's problem is not one of poor image but of bad reality.

WARNING FROM
THE LAST GREAT EMPIRE

The fourth and last test is for America to show that it has heeded the warnings raised by the last great empire to stand where the United States stands today. The history of empires is more than the story of "one damned superpower after another." It is a more complex dance in which each one rises and falls according to its own distinctive faith and foil—its own nationalistic faith and the foil of its own enabling enemy, its legendary Other. Thus the faith of the Greeks was partly in response to the foil of the Persians, that of the Romans to the Carthaginians, that of the Spanish to the Moors, that of the British to the Spanish and French, and that of the Americans at first to the foil of the British and later to that of the Nazis and the Communists, and now to radical Islam.

The trouble in each case is that the double distortion of an overpositive faith combined with an overnegative foil becomes a mirror in which each empire sees only what it wants to see—until it is too late. The lessons of the past are not learned in time. The voices of exceptionalism drown out the voices of conscience. Each empire is therefore an answer to an empire. It liberates itself, then proclaims itself as an empire of liberty, only to become oppressive in its turn. As Christopher Hodgkins commented in his study of the British Empire, it is not uncommon for nations as well as individuals "to be changed through enmity into the image of one's enemy."[23]

America's predecessor as world superpower was the British Empire, which at the dawn of the twentieth century bestrode the world like a colossus and saw itself as an empire of liberty and benevolence. Indeed, historians have argued that its lasting contributions, such as free trade, liberal democracy and the English language, have cast a longer shadow than even the influence of the French and Russian revolutions.

But in the end, none of these "goods" outweighed the bad, and none prevented Britain's slide from dominance to arrogance to complacency to decline and mediocrity, and now to a steady loss of freedom itself (with its lamentable, current erosions of freedom of conscience and free speech, and its encroachments of massive surveillance). The simple fact is that at the height of its power, Britain did not look back and heed the lessons of history. Far from using history to defy history, it ignored history and repeated it.

In a lecture in 1919, classical scholar Gilbert Murray warned that imperial Britain should listen to the voices raised against her in protest around the world. For a start, these voices were neither accidental nor transient, but the latest in the long litany of hatred directed down the centuries against all empires and dominant powers. From "The Burden of Nineveh" to "The Burden of Tyre" to "The Burden of Babylon" to the fall of Rome to the cry of the oppressed against the Ottomans and the Russians, this hatred that is the congealed anger of the oppressed rises up across the years against a long line of oppressive powers. For always there is a yawning chasm between those privileged to live within an empire's borders and those who are treated differently because they are outside.

Further, it is the fate of empires and superpowers to be remembered in the end for their fall as much as their rise and for their vices as much as their virtues—so that "the hatred is at last in part just."[24] They may pride themselves on how they dispense "goods," as Rome did with her *pax Romana*, Spain and France did with their civilization and America does today with her freedom, democracy and capitalism. But none of this matters to their enemies who work long and hard for one thing only—the overthrow of their power.

Finally, Murray warned, each dominant power must face the fact that it sits in its turn where yesterday's hated sat.

> These imperial powers mostly rose to empire not because of their faults, but because of their virtues; because they were strong and competent and trustworthy, and within their borders and among their own people, were mostly models of executive justice. And we think of them as mere types of corruption! The hate they inspired among their subjects has so utterly swamped, in the memory of mankind, the benefits of their good government, or the contented and peaceful lives they made possible to their own peoples. It is an awe-inspiring thought for us who now sit in their place.[25]

More than eighty years before Al Qaeda's attack on the World Trade Center and the stunned American cry, "Why do they hate us?" Murray used the word *Satanism* to describe what was fomenting in the Near East: "the spirit of unmixed hatred toward the existing World Order." "From one end of the Moslem world to the other," he warned in 1919 in an uncanny anticipation of Sayyid Qutb and Osama bin Laden, "there are *Mullahs*, holy men, seeing visions and uttering oracles about another Scarlet Woman who has filled the world with the wine of her abominations."[26]

For all the arrogance, cruelty and ineptness of the British and French meddling in the Middle East over many decades, they did not radicalize Islam as the United States has done in twenty years. Murray's conclusion nearly a century ago therefore challenges America today as much as it did Britain yesterday. He quotes Thucydides: "Not now for the first time have I seen that it is impossible for a Democracy to govern an Empire," and then goes on to echo the words of Burke's speech on the Declaratory Resolution: "There is not a more difficult subject for the understanding of men than to govern a large Empire upon a plan of liberty."[27]

It would be unrealistic to expect the answer to these four tests to be decisive in the course of any single administration. To be an empire worthy of free people is a high and historic challenge, and recent American steps have faltered badly. But the challenge and its consequences are plain for Americans and the world to see. For once again, Americans must never forget: all who aspire to be like Rome in their beginnings must avoid being like Rome at their ending. Rome and its republic fell, and so too will the American republic—unless . . .

7

THE EAGLE AND THE SUN

ANYONE ENTERING THE CENTRAL HALL of George Washington's home at Mount Vernon can hardly fail to see an enormous, oversized, rough iron key in a glass case on the wall. When I visited this elegant Georgian home, the guide did not even mention the key, so I asked her what it was. It was the key to the Bastille, sent to Washington by the Marquis de Lafayette via Thomas Paine in 1790.

The key to the Bastille, "that fortress of despotism" that Lafayette as head of the National Guard ordered razed to the ground early in 1789? Nothing better symbolized the outbreak of the French Revolution, and Lafayette's gift was designed to say just how much the French Revolution owed to the American and that he in particular owed to Washington. "It is a tribute," he wrote in the letter accompanying the key, "Which I owe as A Son to My Adoptive father, as an Aide de Camp to my General, as a missionary of liberty to its patriarch." To which Thomas Paine added his own comment: "That the principles of America opened the Bastile [*sic*] is not to be doubted, and therefore the Key comes to the right place."[1]

ANTIQUARIAN ONLY?

The founders' view of ordered liberty and sustainable freedom is like that key: monumental and heavy with meaning but neglected and only of antiquarian interest to many Americans today. After all, it is feared, such a weight of history must surely lead to pessimism. But is that so, or is the reverse the case, that without the wisdom of the past, there will be no sure way to the future? What will be the outcome when America's story today becomes the history of America tomorrow? Will the United States join the ranks of the superpowers and pay the ransom for its overreach and its neglect of history by falling from power to powerlessness in a generation or two? Or will Americans heed the lessons of history and stave off decline through a genuine movement of renewal?

The happier outcome is the realistic possibility for those who share the founders' hope of sustainable freedom, not to speak of those who hold to the Jewish hope of the possibility of a "return" or the Christian hope of "renewal." But unquestionably the present challenge calls for sustained and serious reflection. It sharpens the need for a frank judgment about sustainable freedom, and it tugs at the elbow of those who dismiss the founders' notion as an antiquarian idea or a pointless luxury.

It was said of Louis XV and his ministers, whose inaction and drift contributed to the pent-up revolutionary forces that swept away his grandson, that they never lost an opportunity to lose an opportunity.

In a similar vein, when Edmund Burke warned William Pitt in a dinner in 1791 that the French Revolution would soon menace other European countries, the prime minister was unperturbed: "Never fear, Mr. Burke, we shall go on as we are until the Day of Judgment."

"Very likely, Sir," Burke replied, "it is the day of no judgment that I am afraid of."[2]

Within a year, the storm clouds Burke saw loomed closer, and Pitt's attitude had changed. In the same way, there are stubborn illusions abroad in America today that only death and history can cure, and there are a thousand tempting dodges through which to duck the challenges. The dream of American-led freedom sweeping the world is the most fatuous of delusions, just as the mentality that pays for the present by mortgaging the future is the most cynical of dodges.

There are countless more modest ways to make a private peace with the present and close one's eyes to the future, but they all end in the same dismal outcome. Some dominant powers indulge a complacent belief in the superiority of their ways until they are too late to act. Others waste a catalog of missed opportunities until they find themselves beyond the point of no return, while others still make too-late and ineffectual reforms that only make matters worse.

Let me state the point bluntly. All who prefer not to pay for their complacency with their liberty and who desire less drastic remedies than death and history must face the fact that America, like Rome and most dominant world powers, will one day decline from within, and that the only alternative to the ironclad decline-after-dominance is *renewal*. So the question no American can afford to avoid is that of the health and condition of America's sustainable freedom.

It is true that ideas and cultures do not have a lifespan and a life cycle as individuals and peoples do. They can be recovered and thrive in different times and different places, just as classical Athenian ideas flourished and were influential in the Renaissance many centuries after they had withered in Greece. Yet there is no question that, just as individual people have a limited lifespan and a discernible life cycle, so do whole nations viewed as peoples. "Never say die" is a magnificent call to indomitable courage, but as a Polyanna-like wish to deny the reality of aging, it is silly. The real challenge, then, is raised to the American people rather than to the founders' ideas themselves. If Americans today have no serious interest in the founders' wisdom and provisions, what are their alternatives? If they have any, they should say so, and they should set out what they are and how they relate to the issues behind the founders' original discussion.

Can the golden triangle of freedom be replaced by a reliance on law, or will law without faith, character and virtue lead only—as it has recently—to an endless proliferation of rules, regulations, laws, lawyers, bureaucracy, litigiousness and prisons, and so inexorably to a loss of freedom?

Can the golden triangle be replaced by technology, or will a reliance on technology without virtue, always under pressure from the TINA principle ("There is no alternative"), lead America from "one nation under God" to "one nation under surveillance" and the sanitized safety of a continent-sized panopticon under the all-seeing eye of closed-circuit cameras?

Will the next generation resolve the culture wars and forge a civil public square within which the full diversity of American voices can make their contribution to sustainable freedom, or will America's current fractious spirit and rancorous bloody-mindedness degenerate into a poisonous and disastrous stalemate?[3]

The answers to these questions are not predetermined, but freedom has its limits, and the illusion that it makes no difference must be sternly refused. Free people are always free to give up freedom in exchange for security. They are *not* free to pretend they are as free as they were before. ("Necessity," Pitt the Younger said, "was the plea for every infringement of human freedom. It was the argument of tyrants: it was the creed of slaves."[4]) Free people are always free to defend their freedom strongly. What they are not free to do is pretend that any and all means of defending freedom are right because they are done in the name of freedom.

If the founders were correct about the need for realism in the light of history, and history since their day has only confirmed their realism, then the one thing Americans cannot do is trust naively that freedom will somehow endure forever—and do nothing or do the wrong thing in the effort to sustain it.

AMERICAN RETURN

I am a strong believer in the future, but only because of an equally strong view of the past. But the wisdom of the past makes for realists, not pessimists, and I strenuously disagree with the common assertion that a candid discussion of decline leads only to nostalgia or despair. There is all the difference between a practical, realistic and concrete return to first things and an idle reverie about a mythic past, let alone an exile's obsession with a waiting-for-Godot hope of going home that will never happen.

I believe emphatically in the possibility of American renewal, and I have solid grounds for my hope. Even when the blind spots of the founders are acknowledged openly, I still believe that the merits of what they accomplished far outweigh the demerits, and I believe too that there is no problem America faces today that cannot be resolved by a strong and determined application of the very real "first things" of the American experiment. Many American ideals and institutions are candidates for such a restoration, but three tasks in particular are essential if durable freedom is to last.

First, America must strongly and determinedly restore civic education, an education that is truly "liberal education," or an education for liberty. Conservatives must get over their shortsighted aversion to the "L word," and liberals must reexplore what liberal education really means and why it matters. As underscored repeatedly, citizens of a free society are born free, but they are not born equal to freedom. To be wise for and worthy of freedom, free citizens need to be educated liberally. Republican habits of the heart do not come with mother's milk; they must be cultivated. The goal, as Milton wrote on behalf of sustaining a "free commonwealth" should be "to make the people fittest to choose, and the chosen fittest to govern."[5]

In comparison with such a vision, the United States has a double problem with American citizenship today, and the combination has become lethal. The lesser and more practical problem, which could be easily remedied with sufficient political will, is that citizenship is not taught adequately in American public schools. But the far greater and more spiritual problem is that citizenship is neither prized nor understood as it should be by American citizens. In the days of the classical Greek republics and the later Italian city republics such as Bologna, citizenship was far more than a matter of domicile or convenience. It was a prized possession handed on from generation to generation like a priceless heirloom, so that citizenship was a priceless privilege and exile was considered a death sentence.

Such a high view of citizenship and civic education was once central to the purpose of America's public schools. It should always be vital to the self-government of citizens, who in turn are vital to the enduring freedom of the republic. Civic education is an essential part of a wider moral education, and like all moral education, it will have to bear on behavior and not simply theory. It will have to address the will and the emotions as well as the mind; it will have to address the common good of the republic as a whole and not just the interests of the individual citizens; and—crucially—it will have to challenge the media and other sources of entertainment whose silent but powerful countereducation is an open contradiction of the liberal education of the key nurturing institutions: the family, the faith community and the school.

There can be legitimate arguments over whether such super-successful television programs as *Survivor* are "good entertainment." But there is no question that their unspoken ethic is lethal to human flourishing and to the challenge of sustaining American republican freedom. The ethics of a survivor and the ethics of a true citizen are antithetical, and one or the other will win in the end—with real consequences.

Unless America succeeds in revaluing citizenship, in restoring civic education and in revitalized education that proves as powerful as the potency of mass entertainment and consumer advertising, the American *unum* will no longer be able to balance the American *pluribus*, and America's freedom itself will continue to wither.

Second, as I have argued more fully elsewhere, America must strongly and determinedly rebuild its civil public square, leading to a profound resolution of the current culture warring and a reopening of public life to people of all faiths and none, so that all citizens are able to play their part in a thriving civil society and a robust democracy.[6]

Unless America succeeds in rebuilding the public square and cultivating a robust civility and "habits of the heart" to balance a reliance on law, public life will remain a battleground for continuing controversies and mounting litigiousness and acrimony; the vitality of America's civil society will be sapped; republican freedom will be crippled; and America will lose its right to be the *novus ordo seclorum*, to stand as "a city on a hill" or to pretend any longer to offer a "true remedy" for the world.

Third, America must strongly and determinedly reorder the grand spheres that make up American society and its powerful cultural influence in the world. A key feature of the modern world is differentiation, the process whereby the modern world reinforces the autonomy of different spheres with their own distinctive ways of thinking and operating: government, the economy, business, education, law, medicine, science and technology, entertainment and so on.

Now, in the global era, these spheres have been given newly expanded fields of operation (such as global markets) and new agencies acting on their behalf (such as multinational corporations). But if each sphere is not checked and balanced, and integrated through a powerful emphasis on ethics in all spheres of life, the result is a dangerous disordering of the spheres. On the one hand, individuals enter the spheres and pursue only their own interests, with no thought for the public good or for the significance of the sphere for the good of the republic. On the other hand, each sphere grows inflated in its self-importance and expands to colonize other spheres—economics turning the whole of life into what can be bought and sold, and politics turning the whole of society into what can be legislated and regulated, and so on.

In short, the founders' commitment to a separation of powers is more vital than ever today, and its current applications must go beyond a worn-out litany of clichés such as "limited government" and "get the government off our backs." The rampant imperialism of the spheres must be reined in, and the citizens' responsibility for the wider common good must be reinforced. Each sphere—business, law, education, entertainment and so on—must be reordered to serve the wider public good, and principles such as individual self-reliance, local self-government and state government must once again be given their proper roles. Not only must the latter be able to balance the dominance of federal government and provide a bulwark against the encroachments of bureaucratic overregulation, they must also carry the robust human and ethical values that can prevent humanity being turned into a global supermarket where even souls are up for sale and profit is the measure of all things.

Unless America succeeds in such a reordering of the spheres, the present imperial hubris of the spheres will continue their runaway inflation, the tutelary state will expand its paternalistic smothering of individual freedom and a politically and economically bloated America will resemble in its star-spangled obesity the enemies of freedom it has resisted so long and so heroically.

Much is made today about "democratic deficits" in the world. More needs to be debated about the role of the excess of state, the surfeit of capitalism and the grand overreach of laws, rules and regulations across the social map. Each of these spheres of society has its own proper role, and each is vital to the American republic, but each must be checked and balanced, and integrated with ethics. The American republic will be sustained only if each sphere attends to its own purpose in the wider role of society, each is properly checked and balanced, and such principles as subsidiarity are respected. Only so will freedom endure beyond the pale liberty of periodic voting to be a way of life that remains self-reliant, self-governing, ordered and long lasting.

To be sure, these restorations do not directly address such immediate and practical challenges as terrorism and the national debt. But they address America's will and capacity to address such tasks, and that is more than half the challenge.

It might also be said that to anyone who reflects on the nature of the American experiment, let alone a foreign admirer, there could hardly be anything simpler, more obvious and more patriotic than these three restorations, especially the first and second. Yet the strange combination of progressive and reactionary forces blocking them is strong and vocal, and so far no leader with sufficient courage and vision has stepped forward to take them on and break the present impasse. With civic education, for example, the clash between backward-looking teachers' unions and forward-looking foundations concerned only for educational "skills" leaves the United States industriously turning out students who are deficient not only in global competitiveness but in American citizenship and in Socrates' examined life.

These three restorations—the renewal of civic education, the restoration of a civil public square, and the re-ordering of the different spheres to serve the common good—must be accompanied by a fourth, which I will not set out here because it is not the business of the republic and emphatically not the responsibility of government. I am referring to a restoration of the integrity and credibility of the faiths and ethics of the citizenry, which in many cases in America today are as faithless, flaccid and fickle as the health of ordered liberty itself. Integrity and order in the spirit of the citizens are as vital as they are in the structures of the commonwealth.

If Lord Acton was right that religion is the key to history and Christopher Dawson was correct that every great culture has been empowered by a vital and creative faith, then as your faiths, so will your character, virtues, and culture be. This means that there is probably no chance of reordering society effectively unless there is a reforming and successful reordering of the faiths of the citizens too. That restoration, however, would require quite separate treatment and lies outside my present concerns.

GOING FORWARD
BY FIRST GOING BACK

The major reason for the present failure to address such basic restorations stems from an irony: *The very notion of restoration needs restoring.* The classical notion of renewal is through a return to the past that is progressive. Herein lies the key difference between cultural progress and scientific progress, for while science builds on the past but never returns to it, cultural progress can be animated by a genuine return to the past. In this sense, contrary to popular misunderstanding, it is possible to turn back the clock.

Of course, the notion of a return to the past is usually dismissed without a thought when progress is considered only on the scientific and technological models, when future-obsession means we are constantly told to reclaim our future (as if we ever possessed it) and when the mindless mantras of innovation and "thinking outside the box" are repeated breathlessly and rarely challenged. No financial instrument, for example, was more innovative (and lucrative) than the packaging of subprime mortgages and credit default swaps, but no one thought to ask whether the innovations were healthy or toxic.

But history shows that when it comes to ideas, it is in fact possible to turn back the clock. Two of the most progressive movements in Western history—the Renaissance and the Reformation—were both the result of a return to the past, though in very different ways and with very different outcomes. The American Revolution itself, in stark contrast to the French, was a conservative revolution—as was the greatness of Benjamin Disraeli's Britain.

The roots of the idea of a return to the past are worth pondering.

What the Jews understood as the national significance of *exodus* and the early American Puritans as the spiritual meaning of *conversion* was paralleled for the founders by the political significance of *revolution*. For all three peoples, though in different ways, the experiences were liberating events that were formative for their creation as distinct new peoples.

Equally, what both the Jews and the early American Puritans understood as the significance of *covenant* was paralleled politically for the founders by the significance of *constitution*. Again, for all three, the achievements were fundamental to the ordering of their lives as liberated peoples.

The third parallel is the forgotten but intriguing one: what the Jews understood by the hope of national renewal through a *return* to the ways of God and the Puritans understood by the hope of renewal through personal and corporate *revival* was paralleled politically in the ideas of the founders. George Mason, characteristically more conservative, spoke of "a frequent recurrence to fundamental first principles," whereas Thomas Jefferson, who was more liberal, spoke of the need for "a revolution every twenty years."[7] Even Machiavelli agreed with this, though sadly not his modern disciples: republics must frequently return to their first principles. "'Things are preserved from destruction by bringing them back to their first principles,' is a rule in Physics; the same holds good in politics."[8]

In other words, all three movements—Jewish, Christian and American—share a striking feature that sets them apart from much modern thinking: *A return to the past can be progressive, not reactionary. Each movement in its own way best goes forward by first going back.* Their innovations were "outside the box" because they were back to basics and not a mindless espousal of the present or a breathless chase after some purported future. The most creative remakings are always through the most faithful rediscoveries.

Put differently, when religious or political beliefs become tired and lose their vigor, the way to reinvigorate them is not to modernize or rebrand them cosmetically, as in Tony Blair's infamous "cool Britannia." The way forward is to return to the source that gave rise to them in the first place. Is the American republic uniquely exempt from the need for such renewal? Or, more to the point, are today's Americans capable of moving beyond boastful complacence to seeking such a restoration? Will an American leader rise with enough humility and courage to lead the way to a wise and robust return to the past? Judged on the evidence of America's recent debates, I will not be holding my breath.

In Plato's *Republic*, Socrates declared that the vitality and endurance of the city they were founding would depend on future leaders holding enough of the same understanding that the founders had when they laid down the founding laws. The same is true of America now, and as I said, I am convinced that America faces no problem today that cannot be resolved through a return to America's first principles. Yet the plain fact is that those who reject the founders' understanding of sustainable freedom are hardly likely to take seriously their views of national and civic renewal, so the folly and madness continue unabated, at least for the moment.

REMISS OF ME

There is no question that in this book I have mapped out a hopeful road. I am not a Pollyanna or a cheerleader or a fan of smiley buttons. But the game is not yet over, and the hour has not quite closed. So this is no time for fear or fear mongering, and the note of hope can and must be raised before the darkness falls.

I will maintain that note of hope until the end, but it would be remiss of me not to underscore that there will be a price—a very steep price—for missing the moment and squandering the opportunity of "the American hour." If justice is not to be denied and if, as Lincoln said in his noble second inaugural address, the judgments of heaven are "true and righteous altogether,"[9] then

America will face the fate of all overreaching empires: the United States will be indicted for its hubris and judged before the world by whether it has lived up to the standard of its own ideals. Then the sorry revelations of a once-proud republic in decline will expose the moral and political contradictions of America just as the malignant revelations of World Wars I and II did for Europe and its hubris.

I am always profoundly moved when I stand before Lincoln's noble words engraved on the wall of his memorial next to him as he sits on his consuls' chair. The torrents of blood "drawn with the sword" in the Civil War, he concluded gravely, were to balance the books on account of "every drop of blood drawn with the lash" of 250 years of slavery. The terrible carnage of the blues and the grays was the severe price paid for the denial of the Declaration of Independence's promise of liberty for all.

Will an equally severe accounting be demanded for America's equally brazen denial of the Declaration's promise of life for all and a myriad of other contradictions of America's declared commitment to freedom? Will there be a moment when the inner contradictions of American republicanism, democracy and capitalism are revealed simultaneously? At least let there be no doubt about the stark alternative to renewal. If there is no American renewal, American dominance can be followed only by American decline. America has reached the point where, apart from restoration, there is no other choice. So let there be no dodging or denial: as America stands before the grave wisdom of Lincoln's "This too shall pass," this is her moment of truth.

Yet even the word *decline* is too gentle. It suggests only a slow, painless slippage, whereas in reality, for empires as well as individuals, though not for nations by themselves, decline is always linked eventually to death. In other words, decline by itself may be a long time coming, so much so that no one believes it will ever come and therefore does not matter. But as the story of empires from Rome to the Soviets demonstrates, the end when it comes is often sudden, shocking and irreversible.

FREEDOM IS THE EAGLE

For those who do care deeply about the future of republican freedom and for those who are open to the possibility of national renewal, let me finish with a reflection on the American symbol—a symbol that never fails to move me as a European. Just as the harp, with its beauty, melody and harmony, is the emblem of my homeland Ireland, so the symbol of the eagle stands for America and for American freedom—and with a power to stir the mind and heart that is beyond words.

The early years of the revolution saw various symbols proposed as America's emblem—from a flight of birds to a flock of sheep to a kettle of fish to a thoroughbred horse to a shaggy buffalo to a wild deer to a black beaver to a coiled rattlesnake. The first committee appointed to the task considered such options as a maiden, a dove, a warrior, a harp, a pillar, a cockerel and two fleurs-de-lis. Benjamin Franklin was notorious as a strong advocate for the wild turkey.[10]

The final choice of the eagle was inspired. Sovereign of the air, with its fierce beak, keen eyes, sharp talons, piercing cry and immense, powerful wings, the eagle rides the winds and commands the heights—the ultimate image of strength, grace and beauty whose soaring flight screams out to watchers on the earth to stand as the sublime symbol of freedom.

Franklin notwithstanding, the choice of the eagle met with widespread approval from the start. In France, the Marquis de Chastellux acclaimed it the perfect picture of the new republic born of such dizzying, high-altitude hopes. Ever eager to score a point over the enemy across the Channel, he wrote to the president of William and Mary College, "It would seem indeed that the English, in all fields, want only half-liberty. Let the owls and bats flutter about in the murky darkness of a feeble twilight; the American eagle must be able to fix its eyes on the sun."[11]

WITH EYES ON THE SUN

With "its eyes on the sun"? The eagle has always represented different things to different people, and so too has the sun. For Franklin, the rising sun was the portent of the rising nation itself, taken from a carving on the back of the chair on which Washington sat during the Philadelphia Convention. For frontiersmen and Native Americans, the eagle had long been the symbol of strength and courage, and an eagle's feather the proud badge of leadership, as in a chief's headdress. For the marquis in France and many in America, the sun toward which the eagle soared was the Enlightenment and the solar energy of its all-triumphant reason.

For many more Americans still, the symbol of the eagle and the sun was biblical. It pointed back to the prophet Isaiah and the strength of those who rise up with eagles' wings because they "wait upon the Lord" (Isaiah 40:31). Just such a biblical eagle had been the figurehead of the *Arbella* that brought John Winthrop and his fellow Puritans to Massachusetts Bay, and the eagle had always been the symbol of St. John and of the Evangelicals.

To be sure, the American eagle has also drawn its critics. Some have assailed it in terms that are closer to Franklin's dismissal of the "disreputable bird," and some have noted that the nation's behavior is unbecoming to an eagle. Mark, in Charles Dickens's *Martin Chuzzlewit*, describes how he would paint the American eagle: "I should want to draw it like a bat for its short-sightedness; like a Bantam for its bragging; like a Magpie, for its honesty; like a Peacock, for its vanity; like an Ostrich, for putting its head in the mud, and thinking nobody sees it."[12]

But far deeper questions arise today. Once America soars higher than any eagle has soared before, does the eagle no longer need the sun? And is there any sun that the high-soaring eagle still recognizes as higher than itself? Is there a reality beyond freedom on which American freedom depends? Those were the questions addressed by G. K. Chesterton after his visit to the United States in 1921 and that was the context of his sober prediction that some "ultimate test" would come. If—as has happened in our postmodern age fourscore years after he wrote—the power of the Jewish and Christian faiths is discarded and the power of the Enlightenment is pronounced dead, what would be the authority that authorizes freedom, human dignity, rights, democracy and, finally, meaning itself? "Men will more and more realize that there is no meaning in democracy if there is no meaning in anything," Chesterton wrote, "and that there is no meaning in anything if the universe has not a centre of significance and an authority that is the author of our rights."[13]

If that day comes, Chesterton warned in words reminiscent of the founders, Americans should ponder the meaning of the symbol of their republic. The eagle is not like owls and bats that fly by night and need no light. Nor is the eagle like kites and vultures whose existence centers only on carrion. No, he wrote in the closing words of his book, "it was far back in the lands of legends, where instincts find their true images, that the cry went forth that freedom is the eagle, whose glory is gazing at the sun."[14]

Freedom is the eagle whose glory is gazing at the sun? No nation rises higher or lasts longer than the great ideas that inspire it. Freedom never lasts forever, because it is harder to be free than not to be free. Freedom must therefore be sustained and not simply won, ordered and taken for granted. American freedom, like American greatness, was not derived from itself, and it cannot be sustained by itself. For the source of its strength it must always look beyond itself.

All of which raises the supreme question for Americans today: Will the eagle cease to fly toward the sun and be grounded? Or will the eagle renew its gaze on the sun and soar again? Always free, will the United States remain free always? That is the standing or falling issue that the present generation faces.

Americans, that is also the form of the question through which you confront three of history's great questions common to all civilizations toward the end of their course: What do you have that you did not receive? What have you done with your inheritance? And what is to be done if you answer the first two questions with honesty?

You are free today to choose the freedom you desire. But with the combined witness of your founders and all history behind you, you are without excuse for the choice you make, and you make it before a watching world and on a global stage. Such is time's sifting of America's character and condition that your choice will not only be America's judgment of itself, but also the judgment of history and of God.

You have turned from your founders and their vision of lasting freedom, and from the deeply held Jewish, Christian and classical beliefs that made their vision both necessary and possible. You have turned to alternative visions of freedom that are seductive but lazy-minded and empty, and are now proving disastrous. And all the time you are turning yourselves into caricatures of your original freedom in ways that are alternatively fascinating and repellent to the world.

Will you return? Will America return? Or will the day soon be here when it is too late and all your efforts are in vain? The shadows are lengthening, and the day of reckoning is near. You have reached a stage that is beyond the cheap illusions of cosmetic makeovers, beyond rebranding and beyond the arts of the spin doctor. Dressed-up destitution deceives no one but the self-deluded.

So let your choice be made, and let it be known. Remember that free societies are rare and transient, that the American republic is neither ancient nor stable and that its nature as a great experiment may not survive the abandonment of the foundation of its founders. Remember also that the worst choice is always the drifters' choice: no choice at all.

It is far better to rise to the challenge of generations past and generations yet unborn, and choose freedom and the faith that it requires, with all their stern requirements as well as their sweet gifts. Is freedom to become America's Achilles' heel or to remain her glory still? Will America go forward strongly by going back wisely?

My hope and prayer is simple: that Americans will do what Rome failed to do and remain a republic not only in name but in reality, a free republic that will remain free across the long marches of time, just as your wisest and most daring once fervently believed that it might.

The Roman republic fell, and later the Roman Empire, but there is no need for America to follow. The watching world stands by to witness what you choose and to see whether your illustrious ancestors will find heirs worthy of their vision. Americans, you are America now, just as the Athenians were Athens and the Romans were Rome. So the choice is yours—and so too will be the consequences. Let your choice be known, and let it be followed through with courage and resolve. Your hour has struck. Your challenge lies before you, and God and the world and history await your answer.

GRATEFUL ACKNOWLEDGMENTS

THIS BOOK HAS HAD A LONGER GESTATION than many of my other books—closer, in fact, to the pregnancy of an elephant. So it would be impossible to mention all the many people to whom I owe a deep debt of gratitude. I would be seriously ungrateful, however, if I did not mention the following:

Mark Rodgers, whose invitation to address the Republican senators at the Governor's Palace in Williamsburg in 2001 was the original spur to the idea behind this book, and who, along with Bill Wichterman, has been a constant source of encouragement and support over the years.

Dr. Robert Cochran, along with Dean Kenneth Starr, whose invitation to give the inaugural lecture at the Nootbaar Institute at the Pepperdine University Law School challenged me to develop the ideas further.

Michael Cromartie, Will Inboden, Dick Ohman and Peggy Wehmeyer, who gave the early draft of the book a trenchant critique that saved me from the many errors and indiscretions that a foreign visitor can easily make.

Erik Wolgemuth, my talented and tireless literary agent, whose willing spirit and indefatigable work were indispensable in bringing this book to the light of printed day.

Al Hsu and his cheerful colleagues at IVP, whom it is truly a pleasure to work with, and Kellie Boyle, whose enthusiasm and expertise have helped launch the book in a way that far exceeded my own capacities.

And above all, to Jenny and CJ, my beloved family, who have lived with this argument from its beginnings and have believed with me though thick and thin that its message deserves to be heard in America today.

Notes

Chapter 1: What Kind of People Do You Think You Are?

[1]Frank L. Kuckhohn, "Churchill Predicts Huge Allied Drive in 1943," *New York Times*, December 27, 1941, p. 1.

[2]Augustine *City of God* 19.24.

[3]Letter of Thomas Jefferson to George Rogers Clark, December 25, 1780, in *The Papers of Thomas Jefferson*, vol. 4 (Princeton, N.J.: Princeton University Press, 2008), pp. 237-38; Letter of Thomas Jefferson to James Madison, April 27, 1809, in James Morton Smith, ed., *The Republic of Letters: The Correspondence between Thomas Jefferson and James Madison, 1776-1826*, vol. 3 (New York: Norton, 1994), p. 1586.

[4]Federalist Paper No. 10, emphasis added.

[5]Montesquieu *The Spirit of Laws* 2.12.1.

[6]Paul A. Rahe, *Soft Despotism, Democracy's Drift: Montesquieu, Rousseau, Tocqueville & the Modern Prospect* (New Haven: Yale University Press, 2009), p. 38.

[7]Ibid.

[8]Montesquieu *Spirit of Laws* 1.4.5.

[9]James Lamont and Simon Rabinovich, "China and India Call for Action," *Financial Times*, November 10, 2011, p. 4.

[10]Paul Barrett, "Wall Street Staggers," *Bloomberg Businessweek*, September 17, 2008, <www.businessweek.com/magazine/content/08_39/b4101000869093.htm>.

[11]"The National Security Strategy of the United States," The White House, September 2002, p. 1, <http://merln.ndu.edu/whitepapers/USnss2002.pdf>.

[12]George W. Bush, Inaugural Address, Washington D.C., January 20, 2005, <http://frwebgate.access.gpo.gov/cgi-bin/getdoc.cgi?dbname=2005_presidential_documents&docid=pd24ja05_txt-13>.

[13]Georg Wilhelm Friedrich Hegel, *The Philosophy of History*, trans. J. Sibree (New York: Wiley, 1944), p. 86.

[14]Niall Ferguson, *Colossus: The Price of America's Empire* (New York: Penguin, 2004), p. 15.

[15]John Milton, "Sonnet XII: I Did but Prompt the Age to Quit Their Clogs," in *Poems* (London: Thomas Dring, 1673).

[16]James Mann, *The China Fantasy: How Our Leaders Explain Away China's Repression* (New York: Viking, 2007), p. 12.

[17]John W. Gardner, *Self-Renewal: The Individual and the Innovative Society* (New York: Norton, 1963), p. 1.

[18]Repeated in personal conversations with the author.

[19]Abraham Lincoln, *Selected Speeches and Writings: Abraham Lincoln* (New York: Vintage, 1992), p. 14.

Chapter 2: Always Free, Free Always

[1]David Hackett Fischer, *Liberty and Freedom* (New York: Oxford University Press, 2005), pp. 1-2, 739.

[2]Alexander Hamilton, *The Papers of Alexander Hamilton* (New York: Columbia University Press, 1961), pp. 121-22.

[3]Letter to Ernest de Chabrol, July 16, 1831, in Paul A. Rahe, *Soft Despotism, Democracy's Drift* (New Haven: Yale University Press, 2009), p. 195.

[4]Machiavelli, *The Discourses on Livy*, trans. Ninian Hill (Digireads.com, 2008), 3.17.

[5]Thomas Hobbes, *Leviathan* (London: George Routledge and Sons, 1889), p. 232.

[6]James Harrington, *Oceana* (Dublin: R. Reilly, 1737).

[7]David McCullough, *1776* (New York: Simon and Schuster, 2005), p. 108.

[8]Ibid., pp. 155, 160.

[9]John Emerich Edward Dalberg-Acton, "Review of Bryce's American Commonwealth," in *Essays in the History of Liberty*, ed. J. Rufus Fears (Indianapolis: Liberty Fund, 1985), p. 404.

[10]Montesquieu *The Spirit of Laws* 1.5.19.

[11]Federalist Paper No. 47.

[12]Jean Jacques Rousseau *On the Social Contract* 1.6.

[13]Hugh Brogan, *Alexis de Tocqueville: A Life* (New Haven: Yale University Press, 2006), p. 184.

[14]Edmund Burke, *On Empire, Liberty, and Reform: Speeches and Letters*, ed. David Bromwich (New Haven: Yale University Press, 2000), p. 81.

[15]James C. Humes, *The Wit and Wisdom of Winston Churchill* (New York: HarperCollins, 1994), p. 183.

[16]Ibid., p. 291.

[17]William Hague, *William Pitt the Younger* (London: HarperCollins, 2004), p. 374.

[18]Burke to Lord Charlemont, August 9, 1789, in Edmund Burke, *Correspondence*, ed. Thomas Copeland (Cambridge: Cambridge University Press, 1968-1978), 6:10.

[19]Marcus Tullis Cicero, "Pro Cluentio," in *The Speeches of Cicero*, trans. H. Grose Hodge, Loeb Classical Library (Cambridge, Mass.: Harvard University Press, 1927), p.379.

[20]George Santayana, *Dominations and Powers: Reflections on Liberty, Society, and Government* (New York: Charles Scribner, 1951), p. 238.

[21]William E. Gladstone, *The Declaration of Independence and the Constitution*, ed. E. Latham (Lexington, Mass.: D. C. Heath, 1976), p. 99; Thomas Jefferson, "Letter to James Madison," November 18, 1788, in *The Papers of Thomas Jefferson*, vol. 15, ed. Julian P. Boyd (Princeton, N.J.: Princeton University Press, 1958), p. 424.

[22]John Emerich Edward Dalberg-Acton, "The American Revolution," in *Essays in the History of Liberty*, ed. J. Rufus Fears (Indianapolis: Liberty Fund, 1985), 1:196-97.

[23]Ibid., p. 35.

[24]Parliamentary History, vol. 29.

[25]Conor Cruise O'Brien, *The Long Affair: Thomas Jefferson and the French Revolution* (London: Pimlico, 1998), p. 102.

[26]Thomas Jefferson to Thomas Paine, September 13, 1789, in Boyd, *Papers of Thomas Jefferson*, vol. 15, p. 424.

[27]O'Brien, *The Long Affair*, p. 42.

[28]Ibid., p. 147.

[29]Ibid., p. 250.

[30]Ibid., p. 249.

[31]Edmund Burke, *Reflections on the Revolution in France* (New York: Penguin Classics, 1982), pp. 89-91.

[32]Montesquieu *The Spirit of Laws* 1.4.8.

[33]Susan Welch et al., *American Government* (Belmont, Calif.: Wadsworth, 2005), p. 37.

[34]Thomas Paine, "The Crisis," in *Common Sense, The Rights of Man, and Other Essential Writings of Thomas Paine* (New York: Meridian, 1984), p. 85.

[35]McCullough, *1776*, p. 68.

[36]Edmund Burke, *Reflections on the Revolution in France*, ed. Frank M. Turner (New Haven: Yale University Press, 2003), p. 7.

[37]Fischer, *Liberty and Freedom*, p. 192.

[38]Lincoln, *Selected Speeches and Writings*, p. 237.

[39]John W. Gardner, *Self-Renewal: The Individual and the Innovative Society* (New York: Norton, 1963), pp. 5, 76.

[40]John Winthrop, "A Model of Christian Charity," in The Journal of John Winthrop 1630-1649 (Cambridge, Mass.: Harvard University Press, 1996), pp. 1-11.

[41]Richard Bauckham, *God and the Crisis of Freedom* (Louisville, Ky.: Westminster John Knox Press, 2002), p. 35.

[42]Isaiah Berlin, *Four Essays on Liberty* (New York: Oxford University Press, 1969), p. 118.

[43]Henry David Thoreau, "15 Feb. 1851," in *The Journal of Henry David Thoreau*, ed. Bradford Torrey and Francis H. Allen (Boston: Houghton Mifflin, 1906), 2:162.

[44]Henry David Thoreau, *Walden and On the Duty of Civil Disobedience* (New York: Collier Books, 1962), p. 51.

[45]Montesquieu *The Spirit of Laws* 2.11.14.

[46]Alexis de Tocqueville, *Democracy in America*, vol. 1 (New York: Vintage, 1990), p. 264.

[47]Montesquieu *The Spirit of Laws* 6.28.41.

Chapter 3: Using History to Defy History

[1]Polybius, *The Histories*, bk. 36, vol. 6, trans. W. R. Paton (Cambridge, Mass.: Harvard University Press, 1927), p. 437.

[2]Ibid.

[3]Livy *History of Rome* 37:35, emphasis added.

[4]Marcus Tullius Ciceronis, *De Amicitia* (White Fish, Mont.: Kessinger, 2004), p. 53.

[5]James Madison, "One Great Respectable and Flourishing Empire," in Federalist Paper No. 14, 30 November 1787, ed. Terence Ball (Cambridge: Cambridge University Press, 2003), p. 63.

[6]Ibid.

[7]Russell Kirk, *Eliot and His Age: T. S. Eliot's Moral Imagination in the Twentieth Century* (Wilmington, Del.: Intercollegiate Studies Institute, 2008), p.18.

[8]Letter to Louis de Kergorlay, 10 November 1836, in Paul A. Rahe, *Soft Despotism, Democracy's Drift* (New Haven: Yale University Press, 2009), p. 154.

[9]Kirk, *Eliot and His Age*, p. 52.

[10]Letter to artist John Trumbull, 15 February 1789, in *Jefferson: Writings*, ed. Merrill Peterson (New York: Library of America, 1984).

[11]Neil Postman, *Amusing Ourselves to Death* (New York: Viking Penguin, 1985), pp. 136-37.

[12]Montesquieu *De l'esprit des lois* 6.30.14.

[13]Goethe, *West-Oestliche Divan*, section 5, *Buch des Unmuts*.

[14]Hugh Brogan, *Alexis de Tocqueville: A Life* (New Haven: Yale University Press), p. 93.

[15]Chris Wrigley, *Winston Churchill: A Biographical Companion* (Santa Barbara, Calif.: ABC-CLIO, 2002), p. xxiv.

[16]Ted Hughes, "Hear it again," *New Library: The People's Network*, 1998, <www.ukoln.ac.uk/services/lic/newlibrary/poem.html>.

[17]Patrick Henry, "Speech on a Resolution to Put Virginia into a State of Defence," in *American Patriotism: Speeches, Letters, and Other Papers Which Illustrate the Foundation, the Development, the Preservation of the United States*, ed. Selim H. Peabody (New York: American Book Exchange, 1880), p. 108.

[18]Polybius *Histories* 4.57.

[19]George Washington, "September 17, 1796, Farewell Address," George Washington Papers at the Library of Congress, 1741-1799: Series 2 Letterbooks, Letterbook 24, <http://memory.loc.gov/cgi-bin/ampage?collId=mgw2&fileName=gwpage024.db&recNum=228>.

[20]Abraham Lincoln, "Speech to the Young Men's Lyceum of Springfield," 27 January 1838, in *This Fiery Trial: The Speeches and Writings of Abraham Lincoln*, ed. William E. Gienapp (New York: Oxford University Press, 2002), p. 10.

[21]Kenneth N. Waltz, "Structural Realism After the Cold War," in *America Unrivalled: The Future of the Balance of Power*, ed. G. John Ikenberry (Ithaca, N.Y.: Cornell University Press, 2002), p. 53.

[22]Stephen N. Walt, "Keeping the World 'Off-Balance,'" in *American Unrivaled*, p. 154.

[23]Polybius *Histories* 1.6.

[24]Ibid.

[25]Ibid.

[26]Ibid.

[27]Ibid.

[28]Anthony Everitt, *Cicero: The Life and Times of Rome's Greatest Politician* (New York: Random House, 2001), p. 98.

[29]Montesqieu *The Spirit of Laws* 1.8.5.

[30]Ibid., 1.7.4.

[31]Ibid., 1.2.2.

[32]John W. Gardner, *Self-Renewal: The Individual and the Innovative Society* (New York: Norton, 1963), p. 116.

[33]Paul Virilio, *Speed and Politics*, trans. Marc Polizotti (Los Angeles: Semiotext(e), 2006), p. 158.

[34]Isaiah 40:6; Sultan Mehmet, in John Freely, *Istanbul: The Imperial City* (London: Penguin, 1996), p. 177; Dante, in *La Vita Nuova*, bk. 23, trans. Dante Gabriel Rossetti (Mineola, N.Y.: Dover, 2001), p. 24.

[35]Seneca, *On the Shortness of Life* (New York: Penguin, 2005), p. 1.

[36]"A Broken Appointment," in Claire Tomalin, *Thomas Hardy: The Time-Torn Man* (London: Penguin, 2006), p. 249.

[37]Seneca, *Shortness*, p. 25.

[38]Cicero *Treatise on the Commonwealth* 5.

[39]John Emerich Edward Dalberg-Acton, *Essays in the History of Liberty*, ed. J. Rufus Fears (Indianapolis: Liberty Fund, 1985), p. 20.

[40]Edward Gibbon, *The History of the Decline and Fall of the Roman Empire* (London: The Folio Society, 1990), p. 333.

[41]Ibid., p. 334.

[42]Abraham Lincoln, "Address Before the Young Men's Lyceum," 1838, in *This Fiery Trial*, p. 13.

[43]Abraham Lincoln, *Selected Speeches and Writings: Abraham Lincoln* (New York: Vintage Books, 1992), p. 237.

[44]Michael B. Oren, *Power, Faith, and Fantasy: America in the Middle East 1776 to the Present* (New York: Norton, 2007), p. 253.

[45]Ibid., p. 237.

[46]Walter Lippmann, *The Public Philosophy* (New York: Mentor Books, 1955), pp. 74-75.

[47]Niall Ferguson, *Colossus: The Price of America's Empire* (New York: Penguin, 2004), p. 34.

[48]Charles Newton Wheeler, "Fight to Disarm His Life's Work, Henry Ford Vows," *Chicago Daily Tribune*, May 25, 1916.

[49]Joseph Conrad, *Nostromo: A Tale of the Seaboard* (New York: Oxford University Press, 1984), p. 76.

[50]Wendell Berry, *Sex, Economy, Freedom and Community* (New York: Pantheon Books, 1993), p. xiv.

Chapter 4: The Golden Triangle of Freedom

[1]Carol Berkin, "George Washington and the Newburgh Conspiracy," in *I Wish I Had Been There*, ed. Byron Hollenshead (New York: Doubleday, 2006), p. 38.

[2]William Safire, ed., *Lend Me Your Ears: Great Speeches in History* (New York: Norton, 1997), p. 96.

[3]Berkin, "George Washington," p. 49.

[4]Montesqieu *The Spirit of Laws* 6.28.41.

[5]Thomas Jefferson, "Letter to George Washington," 16 April 1784, in *The Papers of Thomas Jefferson*, vol. 18:4, ed. Julian P. Boyd (Princeton, N.J.: Princeton University Press, 1971), p. 397.

[6]Ashton Applewhite, ed., *And I Quote* (New York: Thomas Dunne Books, 2003), p. 268.

[7]Gore Vidal, *Inventing a Nation: Washington, Adams, and Jefferson* (New Haven: Yale University Press, 2003), p. 3.

[8]Henry Lee, "Speech delivered to the U.S. Congress on George Washington's Death," 14 December 1799, in Frank E. Grizzard Jr., *George! A Guide to All Things Washington* (Charlottesville, Va.: Mariner Publishing, 2005), p. 110.

[9]John Adams, "Reply to Congress After Washington's Death," 23 December 1799, in *The Wisdom of John Adams*, ed. Kees de Mooy (New York: Citadel, 2003), p. 254.

[10]Henry Cabot Lodge, ed., *The Works of Alexander Hamilton*, vol. 2 (New York: G. P. Putnam, 1904), p. 444.

[11]John Gray, *Heresies: Against Progress and Other Illusions* (London: Granta Books, 2005), p. 145.

[12]Thomas Jefferson, "Letter to James Madison," 6 September 1789, in *Our Sacred Honor*, ed. William J. Bennett (New York: Simon and Schuster, 1997), p. 342.

[13]Learned Hand, "The Spirit of Liberty" speech in Central Park, 21 May 1944, in Learned Hand, *The Spirit of Liberty: Papers and Addresses*, ed. Irving Dilliard (New York: Knopf, 1963).

[14]Machiavelli, *Discourses on Livy*, trans. Harvey C. Mansfield and Nathan Tarcov (Chicago: University of Chicago Press, 1998), p. 5.

[15]Machiavelli, *The Prince and Other Writings*, trans. Wayne A. Rebhorn (New York: Barnes & Noble Classics, 2003), section 15.

[16]Paul A. Rahe, *Republics Ancient and Modern: Classical Republicanism and the American Revolution* (Chapel Hill: University of North Carolina Press, 1992), p. 17.

[17]In *The Papers of Alexander Hamilton*, vol. 3, p. 103, *The Continentalist*, no. 6 (July 4, 1782).

[18]T. S. Eliot, *The Rock* (New York: Harcourt Brace, 1934).

[19]Montesquieu *The Spirit of Laws* 1.3.6.

[20]Bernard Mandeville, *Fable of the Bees* (Charleston, S.C.: Nabu Press, 2010), 1.47.51.

[21]Bernard Bailyn, *To Begin the World Anew: The Genius and Ambiguities of the American Framers* (New York: Alfred A. Knopf, 2003), p. 34.

[22]Lord Moulton, "Law and Manners," *The Atlantic*, July 1924.

[23]Edmund Burke, "First Letter on Regicidal Peace," in *The Wisdom of Edmund Burke: Extracts from His Speeches and Writings*, ed. Edward Pankhurst (London: John Murray, 1886), p. 171.

[24]Rousseau *The Social Contract* 2.12.

[25]Hugh Brogan, *Alexis de Tocqueville: A Life* (New Haven: Yale University Press), p. 272.

[26]Josiah Quincy, *Memoir of the Life of John Quincy Adams* (Philadelphia: Crosby, Nichols, and Lee, 1860), p. 111.

[27]James Madison, debate in the Federal Convention, 4 June 1787, in *The Papers of James Madison*, vol. 2, ed. Henry D. Gilpin (Washington, D.C.: Langtree & Sullivan, 1840), p. 805.

[28]Ariel Sabar, "Too Much Religion on Campaign Trail?" *Christian Science Monitor*, 28 December 2007, <www.csmonitor.com/2007/1228/p02s01-uspo.html>.

[29]Benjamin Franklin, Letter, 17 April 1787, in *The Works of Benjamin Franklin*, ed. Jared Sparks (Chicago: Townsend Mac County, 1882), p. 287.

[30]David Hacket Fischer, *Liberty and Freedom* (New York: Oxford University Press, 2005), p. 185.

[31]John Adams to Zabdiel Adams, 21 June 1776, in C. F. Adams, *Works*, vol. 10 (New York: Little, Brown, 1856), p. 401.

[32]Letter to Mercy Otis Warren, 16 April 1776, *Papers of John Adams*, vol. 4, pp. 124-25, ed. Robert J. Taylor, Gregg L. Lint and Celeste Walker (Cambridge, Mass.: Harvard University Press, 1979).

[33]Virginia Declaration of Rights, 1776, <www.gunstonhall.org/georgemason/human_rights/vdr_final.html>.

[34]Edwin Gaustad, *Faith of the Founders* (Waco, Tex.: Baylor University Press, 2004); James Hutson, *The Founders on Religion* (Princeton, N.J.: Princeton University Press, 2005).

[35]Letter to Claude Francois de Rivarol, 1 June 1791, in *The Correspondence of Edmund Burke*, ed. Thomas W. Copeland (Chicago: University of Chicago Press, 1958-1978), 6:265-70.

[36]George Washington, "First Inaugural Address," 30 April 1789, in David Ramsay, *The Life of George Washington* (Baltimore: Joseph Jewett and Cushing & Sons, 1832), p. 177.

[37]John Adams, Diary, 2 June 1778, *Diary and Autobiography of John Adams, Volumes 1-4: Diary (1755-1804) and Autobiography (through 1780)*, ed. L. H. Butterfield, Leonard C. Faber and Wendell D. Garrett (Cambridge, Mass.: Belknap, 1961).

[38]John Adams, "A Dissertation on the Canon and Feudal Law," in *The Political Writings of John Adams*, ed. George W. Carey (Washington, D.C.: Regnery Publishing, 2000), p. 13.

[39]Paul A. Rahe, *Montesquieu and the Logic of Liberty* (New Haven: Yale University Press, 2009), p. 36.

[40]Paul Woodruff, *First Democracy: The Challenge of an Ancient Idea* (Oxford: Oxford University Press, 2005), p. 69.

[41]Albert Camus, *The Myth of Sisyphus and Other Essays* (New York: Alfred A. Knopf, 1967), p. 66.

[42]George Reedy, *The Twilight of the Presidency* (New York: World Publishing, 1970), p. 20.

[43]Len Colodny and Tom Shachtman, *The Forty Year War—The Rise and Fall of the Neocons, from Nixon to Obama* (New York: HarperCollins, 2009), p. 158.

[44]James Q. Wilson, *On Character* (Washington, D.C.: American Enterprise Institute Press, 1995), p. 23.

[45]John Adams, "Letter to Zabdiel Adams," 21 June 1776, in *Letters of Delegates to Congress, 1774-1779*, ed. Paul H. Smith (Washington, D.C.: Library of Congress, 1976).

[46]John Witherspoon, "The Dominion of Providence over the Passions of Men," in *Political Sermons of the American Founding Era: 1783-1805*, ed. Ellis Sandoz (Indianapolis: Liberty Fund, 1998).

[47]Ibid.

[48]George Washington, "September 17, 1796, Farewell Address."

[49]Ibid.

[50]Brogan, *Alexis de Tocqueville*, p. 320.

[51]Alexis de Tocqueville, *Democracy in America*, vol. 3, ed. Eduardo Nolla, trans. James T. Schleifer (Indianapolis: Liberty Fund, 2010).

[52]Benjamin Rush, "Letter to John Adams," in *Our Sacred Honor*, ed. William J. Bennett (New York: Simon and Schuster, 1997), p. 88.

[53]David A. Wilson, *Paine and Cobbett: The Transatlantic Connection* (Montreal: McGill-Queen's University Press, 1988), p. 178.

⁵⁴Benjamin Franklin, "Letter to Unknown," 3 July 1786, in *The Writings of Benjamin Franklin*, vol. 9, ed. Albert Henry Smyth (New York: Macmillan, 1906), p. 522.

⁵⁵George Washington, *Maxims of George Washington* (New York: Appleton, 1894), p. 341.

⁵⁶John Adams, "Address to the Military," 11 October 1798, in William J. Federer, *America's God and Country: Encyclopedia of Quotations* (Coppell, Tex.: Fame Publishing, 1994), p. 10.

⁵⁷John Jay, "Address to the American Bible Society, May 9, 1822," *The Correspondence and Public Papers of John Jay* (New York: G. P. Putnam's Sons, 1794), 4:484.

⁵⁸O. E. Fuller, *Brave Men and Women: Their Struggles, Failures, and Triumphs* (Chicago: H. J. Smith, 1884), pp. 42-43.

⁵⁹David Waldstreicher, ed., *Notes on the State of Virginia* (New York: Palgrave, 2002), p. 195.

⁶⁰James Madison, "Speech in the Virginia Ratifying Convention," 20 June 1788, in *Advice to My Country* (Charlottesville: University of Virginia Press, 1997), p. 24.

⁶¹Alexander Hamilton, *The Works of Alexander Hamilton*, ed. Henry Cabot Lodge (New York: G. P. Putnam, 1904), p. 277.

⁶²Benjamin Franklin, "Letter to Ezra Stiles," 1 March 1790, in *Autobiography and Other Writings*, ed. Ormond Seavey (New York: Oxford University Press, 1993), p. 353.

⁶³Rahe, *Republics Ancient and Modern*, p. 753.

⁶⁴Washington, "September 17, 1796, Farewell Address."

⁶⁵Thomas Jefferson, letter to James Smith on December 8, 1822, *Memoir, correspondence, and miscellanies from the papers of T. Jefferson* (Charlottesville, Va.: F. Carr, 1829), p. 360.

⁶⁶Roger Williams, "The Bloudy Tenent of Persecution," in Romeo Elton, *The Life of Roger Williams* (New York: Putnam, 1852), p. 67.

⁶⁷James Madison, "Memorial and Remonstrance," in *The Mind of the Founder: Sources of the Political Thought of James Madison*, ed. Marvin Myers (Waltham, Mass.: Brandeis University Press, 1981), p. 8.

⁶⁸John Adams, "Letter to John Quincy Adams," 16 June 1816, in Hutson, *Founders on Religion*, p. 20.

⁶⁹Alexander Hamilton, "The Stand III," 7 April 1798, in *The Papers of Alexander Hamilton* (New York: Columbia University Press, 1974), 21:402.

⁷⁰Gertrude Himmelfarb, *The Roads to Modernity: The British, French, and American Enlightenments* (New York: Alfred A. Knopf, 2004), p. 155.

⁷¹In Hutson, *Founders on Religion*, p. 96.

⁷²Bailyn, *To Begin the World Anew*, p. 49.

⁷³Dalberg-Acton, *Essays*, p. 30.

⁷⁴Ibid., p. 93.

⁷⁵See Hutson, *Founders on Religion*, p. 165.

⁷⁶Williams, "The Bloudy Tenent," p. 66-67.

⁷⁷Madison, "Memorial and Remonstrance." Following quotes refer to this work as well.

⁷⁸John Leland, "The Rights of Conscience Inalienable," in *The American Republic: Primary Sources*, ed. Bruce Frohnen (Indianapolis: Liberty Fund, 2002), p. 80.

⁷⁹Thomas L. Friedman, "Budgets of Mass Destruction," *New York Times*, 1 February

2004, <www.nytimes.com/2004/02/01/opinion/budgets-of-mass-destruction.html?scp=
1&sq=budgets%20of%20mass%20destruction&st=cse>.

[80]Peter L. Berger, "The Serendipity of Liberties," in *The Structure of Freedom: Correlations, Causes, and Cautions,* ed. Richard John Neuhaus (Grand Rapids: Eerdmans, 1991), p. 16.

[81]Rodney Stark, *One True God: The Historical Consequences of Monotheism* (Princeton, N.J.: Princeton University Press, 2001), p. 61, emphasis in original.

[82]See Os Guinness, *The Case for Civility—and Why Our Future Depends on It* (San Francisco: HarperOne, 2008).

[83]Letter to Edward Everett, March 2, 1819, in *The Writings of James Madison,* vol. 9, ed. Gaillard Hunt (New York: Putnam, 1900-1910), pp. 124-34.

[84]William Lee Miller, *First Liberty: Religion and the American Republic* (New York: Alfred A. Knopf, 1986), p. 143.

Chapter 5: The Completest Revolution of All

[1]John Lukacs, *Outgrowing Democracy: A History of the United States in the Twentieth Century* (New York: Doubleday, 1984), p. 140.

[2]See, for example, Jürgen Habermas, *The Divided West* (Cambridge: Polity Press, 2006).

[3]Robert Kagan, *Of Paradise and Power: America and Europe in the New World Order* (New York: Alfred A. Knopf, 2003), p. 3.

[4]George Weigel, *The Cube and the Cathedral: Europe, America, and Politics Without God* (New York: Basic Books, 2005).

[5]Alexis de Tocqueville, *Democracy in America,* vol. 1, trans. Henry Reeve (New York: Vintage Books, 1990), 2.Ii.9.

[6]James Bryce, *The American Commonwealth,* vol. 2 (Indianapolis: Liberty Fund, 1995), p. 563, emphasis added.

[7]G. K. Chesterton, *What I Saw in America* (London: Hodder and Stoughton, 1922), chap. 19.

[8]Niall Ferguson, *Colossus: The Price of America's Empire* (New York: Penguin, 2004), p. 54.

[9]John Adams, "Discourses on Davila," in *The Political Writings of John Adams,* ed. George W. Carey (Washington, D.C.: Regnery Publishing, 2000), pp. 361-62.

[10]Thomas Jefferson, "First Inaugural Address," March 4, 1801, *The Papers of Thomas Jefferson,* Volume 33: 17 February to 30 April 1801 (Princeton, N.J.: Princeton University Press, 2006), pp. 143-48.

[11]Thomas Jefferson, *Notes on the State of Virginia* (New York: Harper Torchbook, 1964), p. 152.

[12]Paul A. Rahe, *Soft Despotism, Democracy's Drift* (New Haven: Yale University Press, 2009), p. 249.

[13]See Os Guinness, *The Case for Civility—And Why Our Future Depends on It* (San Francisco: HarperOne, 2008).

[14]Philip Rieff, *My Life Among the Deathworks: Sacred Order/Social Order* (Charlottesville: University of Virginia Press, 2006), 1:14.

[15]Philip Rieff, "Toward a Theory of Culture," in *The Jew of Culture: Freud, Moses, and*

Modernity, ed. Arnold M. Eisen and Gideon Lewis-Kraus (Charlottesville: University of Virginia Press, 2008), p. 88.

[16]Samuel P. Huntingdon, *Who Are We? Challenges to America's National Identity* (New York: Simon & Schuster, 2005), p. 272.

[17]Eric Foner, *The Story of American Freedom* (New York: Norton, 1998), p. 97, emphasis added.

[18]Abraham Heschel, *Who Is Man?* (Stanford, Calif.: Stanford University Press, 1965), p. 97.

[19]Alexis de Tocqueville, *The Old Regime and the Revolution*, vol. 1, ed. Francois Furet and Francoise Melonio (Chicago: University of Chicago Press, 1998), p. 7.

[20]In James L. Heft, ed., *A Catholic Modernity? Charles Taylor's Marianist Award Lecture* (Oxford: Oxford University Press, 1999), p. 113.

[21]Michel Houellebecq, *The Elementary Particles* (New York: Vintage Books, 2001).

[22]G. K. Chesterton, *Orthodoxy* (Chicago: Moody Publishers, 2009), p. 64.

[23]Isaiah Berlin, *Four Essays on Liberty* (New York: Oxford University Press, 1969), p. 122.

[24]Montesquieu *The Spirit of Laws* 2.11.4. 2.

[25]Berlin, *Four Essays*, p. 147.

[26]John Lord Acton, *The Roman Question*, Rambler 2nd new series 2 (January 1860), p. 146.

[27]Pico della Mirandola, "Oration on the Dignity of Man," in *The Portable Renaissance Reader*, ed. J. B. Ross and M. M. McLaughlin (New York: Penguin, 1977), pp. 476-79.

[28]Quote in Kenneth Clark, *Civilization* (London: John Murray, 1971), p. 104.

[29]Emil Brunner, *Christianity and Civilisation*, Part 1 (London: Nisbet, 1947), p. 134.

[30]Friedrich Nietzsche, *Thus Spake Zarathustra* (New York: Macmillan, 1896), p. 116.

[31]Herbert Spencer, *Social Statics* (London: Williams & Norgate, 1892), p. 32.

[32]Walt Whitman, "Leaves of Grass," in *Complete Poetry and Collected Prose*, ed. Justin Kaplan (New York: Library of America, 1982), p. 165.

[33]Julian Huxley, ed., *The Humanist Frame* (London: George Allen & Unwin, 1961), p. 7.

[34]John F. Kennedy, "A Strategy of Peace." Lecture delivered at American University, Washington D.C., June 10, 1963.

[35]John Gray, *Straw Dogs: Thoughts on Humans and Other Animals* (New York: Farrar, Straus and Giroux, 2007), p. 5.

[36]Ayn Rand, *Virtue of Selfishness: A New Concept of Egoism* (New York: New American Library, 1964), p. 27.

[37]Bacon *Novum Organum* 1.88, 1.116, 1.129; and Bacon *Of the Advancement of Learning* 1.7.33, 2.21.

[38]Gray, *Straw Dogs*, p. 31.

[39]Heft, *A Catholic Modernity?* p. 29.

[40]Ayn Rand, *The Fountainhead* (New York: New American Library, 1943), p. 686.

[41]Benjamin R. Barber, *Consumed: How Markets Corrupt Children, Infantilize Adults, and Swallow Citizens Whole* (New York: Norton, 2008), p. 117.

[42]Wilfred M. McClay, *The Masterless: Self and Society in Modern America* (Chapel Hill: University of North Carolina Press, 1994), p. 4.

[43]Tocqueville, *Democracy in America*, 2:106.

[44]Joseph Cardinal Ratzinger, *Europe Today and Tomorrow* (San Francisco: Ignatius Press, 2007), p. 29.

[45]Dale Kuehne, *Sex and the I-World: Rethinking Relationship in an Age of Individualism* (Grand Rapids: Baker Academic, 2009), p. 43.

[46]Tocqueville, *Democracy in America*, 2.4.6.

[47]Ibid.

[48]Ibid., 1.4.13

[49]Paul A. Rahe, *Montesquieu and the Logic of Liberty* (New Haven: Yale University Press, 2009), p. 39.

Chapter 6: An Empire Worthy of Free People

[1]Rudyard Kipling, "Recessional," in *Rudyard Kipling: Selected Poems*, ed. Jan Hewitt (London: Orion Publishing, 2003), p. 1805.

[2]Paul A. Rahe, *Soft Despotism, Democracy's Drift: Montesquieu, Rousseau, Tocqueville & the Modern Prospect* (New Haven: Yale University Press, 2009), p. 7.

[3]Ibid.

[4]"Remarks on the Policy of the Allies with Respect to France," *The Works of Edmund Burke* (Boston: Little, Brown, 1901), 4.457.

[5]See Niall Ferguson, *Colossus: The Price of America's Empire* (New York: Penguin, 2004), p. xv.

[6]Ibid., p. 64.

[7]Anthony Pagden, *Peoples and Empires* (New York: Modern Library, 2001), p. 86.

[8]Joseph Conrad, *Heart of Darkness* (Harmondsworth, U.K.: Penguin, 1989), p. 32.

[9]Pagden, *Peoples and Empires*, p. xxiii.

[10]Ferguson, *Colossus*, p. xxv.

[11]Pagden, *Peoples and Empires*, p. 35.

[12]Thomas More, *Utopia*, trans. Paul Turner (Harmondsworth, U.K.: Penguin, 1965), pp. 58-59.

[13]Ibid.

[14]Pagden, *Peoples and Empires*, p. 14.

[15]Ferguson, *Colossus*, pp. 209, 211-12.

[16]Ibid., p. 295.

[17]Samuel Johnson, *The Yale Edition of the Works of Samuel Johnson* (New Haven: Yale University Press, 1958), 10:150.

[18]Pagden, *Peoples and Empires*, p. 134.

[19]Ferguson, *Colossus*, p. 228.

[20]John Pilger, *Freedom Next Time* (London: Bantam Press, 2006), p. 16.

[21]Robert Ferrell, ed., *Off the Record: The Private Papers of Harry S. Truman* (Columbia: University of Missouri Press, 1997), p. 310.

[22]Peter Singer, *One World: The Ethics of Globalization* (Melbourne: Text Publishing, 2002), p. 217.

[23]Christopher Hodgkins, *Reforming Empire: Protestant Colonialism and Conscience in British Literature* (Columbia: University of Missouri Press, 2002), p. 74.

[24]Gilbert Murray, "Satanism and the World Order," in *Humanist Essays* (London: Unwin Books 1964), p. 198.

[25]Ibid.

[26]Ibid.

[27]Ferguson, *Colossus*, p. xxv.

Chapter 7: The Eagle and the Sun

[1]Christine H. Messing, John B. Rudder and Diane Windham Shaw, *A Son and His Adoptive Father* (Alexandria, Va.: Mount Vernon Ladies Association, 2006).

[2]William Hague, *William Pitt the Younger* (London: HarperCollins, 2004), p. 290.

[3]See Os Guinness, *The Case for Civility—and Why Our Future Depends on It* (San Francisco: HarperOne, 2008).

[4]Ibid., p. 140.

[5]John Milton, "The Ready and Easy Way to Establish a Free Commonwealth," *The Prose Works of John Milton* (London: H. G. Bohn, 1848), 2:126.

[6]See Guinness, *Case for Civility*.

[7]Garry Wills, *Inventing America: Jefferson's Declaration of Independence* (New York: Houghton Mifflin Harcourt, 2002), p. 124.

[8]Niccolo Machiavelli, quoted in Francis Bacon, "Of the Dignity and Advancement of Learning," *The Works of Francis Bacon*, vol. VII, trans. James Spedding (New York: Hurd and Houghton, 1869), p. 473.

[9]Abraham Lincoln, "Second Inaugural Address." Given in Washington, D.C., March 4, 1865.

[10]David Hackett Fischer, *Liberty and Freedom* (New York: Oxford University Press, 2005), pp. 148-49.

[11]Ibid., p. 149.

[12]Charles Dickens, *Martin Chuzzlewit* (London: Macmillan, 1954), chap. 34.

[13]G. K. Chesterton, *What I Saw in America* (New York: Da Capo Press, 1968), p. 308.

[14]Ibid.

Name Index

Subject Index